Information Security Analytics

Information Security Analytics

Finding Security Insights, Patterns, and Anomalies in Big Data

Mark Ryan M. Talabis

Robert McPherson

I. Miyamoto

Jason L. Martin

D. Kaye, Technical Editor

Amsterdam • Boston • Heidelberg • London
New York • Oxford • Paris • San Diego
San Francisco • Singapore • Sydney • Tokyo
Syngress is an Imprint of Elsevier

Acquiring Editor: *Chris Katsaropoulos*
Editorial Project Manager: *Benjamin Rearick*
Project Manager: *Punithavathy Govindaradjane*
Designer: *Matthew Limbert*

Syngress is an imprint of Elsevier
225 Wyman Street, Waltham, MA 02451, USA

Notices
Knowledge and best practice in this field are constantly changing. As new research and
experience broaden our understanding, changes in research methods, professional
practices, or medical treatment may become necessary.

Practitioners and researchers must always rely on their own experience and knowledge
in evaluating and using any information, methods, compounds, or experiments
described herein. In using such information or methods they should be mindful
of their own safety and the safety of others, including parties for whom they have a
professional responsibility.

To the fullest extent of the law, neither the Publisher nor the authors, contributors, or
editors, assume any liability for any injury and/or damage to persons or property as a
matter of products liability, negligence or otherwise, or from any use or operation of
any methods, products, instructions, or ideas contained in the material herein.

ISBN: 978-0-12-800207-0

British Library Cataloguing in Publication Data
A catalogue record for this book is available from the British Library

Library of Congress Cataloging-in-Publication Data
A catalogue record for this book is available from the Library of Congress

For information on all Syngress publications visit
our website at http://store.elsevier.com/Syngress

Working together
to grow libraries in
developing countries

www.elsevier.com • www.bookaid.org

Dedication

This book is dedicated to Joanne Robles, Gilbert Talabis, Hedy Talabis, Iquit Talabis, and Herbert Talabis.

Ryan

I would like to dedicate this book to my wife, Sandy, and to my sons, Scott, Chris, Jon, and Sean. Without their support and encouragement, I could not have taken on this project. I owe my dog, Lucky, a debt of gratitude as well. He knew just when to tell me I needed a hug break, by putting his nose under my hands, and lifting them off the keyboard.

Robert

This book is dedicated to my friends, my family, my mentor, and all the dedicated security professionals, who tirelessly work to secure our systems.

I. Miyamoto

Contents

Foreword

The information security field is a challenging one accompanied with many unsolved problems and numerous debates on solving such problems. In contrast to other fields such as physics, astronomy and similar sciences this one hasn't had a chance to be succumbed to scrupulous theoretical reviews before we find these problems dramatically affecting the world we live in. The Internet is the proving grounds for security research and it's a constant battle to stay appropriately defended against the offensive research that is conducted on this living virtual organism. There are a lot of industry hype out there convoluting the true tradecraft of information security, and more specifically in regards to "analytics" and "Big Data" and then this book hits the shelves essentially in an effort to truly enlighten the audience on what the genuine value is gained when applying data science to enhance your security research. This informative tome is not meant to be quickly read and understood by the average audience, but instead this book rightfully deserves the audience of researchers and security practitioners dedicated to their work and who seek to apply it in a practical and preemptive way to apply data science to solve increasingly difficult information security problems.

Talabis, McPherson, Miyamoto, and Martin are the perfect blend together and they deliver such fascinating knowledge throughout this book, demonstrating the applicability of analytics to all sorts of problems that affect businesses and organizations across the globe. I remember in 2010 when I was working at Damballa that data science, machine learning, statistics, correlations, and analysis were all being explored in our research department. It was exciting times – the R Language was getting popular around then and a hint of a new chapter for information security was about to begin. Well it did… but a lot of marketing buzzwords also got pushed through and so now we have "Security Analytics" and "Big Data" and "Threat Intelligence" and of course… "Cyber" with no real meanings to anyone … until now.

"Information Security Analytics" is one of the few technical books I've read that I can say I directly started applying what I had learned from the book into my work I do with my team. This book also introduces more proactive insights into solving these problems by dedication to the pure research aspects of the information security field. This is much better than what we have been doing these days with reliance upon just operational answers such as SIEM, Threat Feeds and basic correlation and analysis. My job involves Cyber Counterintelligence research work with the number one big four consulting firm in the world and the value of data science and pure security research is just being tapped into and recognized, but with this book on our shelf I have no doubt the knowledge offered within these chapters will take my team and the firm as a whole to another level.

I leave you with that and it is with great honor that I say...
Sincerely, enjoy the book!

Lance James
Head of Cyber Intelligence
Deloitte & Touche LLP

About the Authors

Mark Ryan M. Talabis is the Chief Threat Scientist of Zvelo Inc. Previously, he was the Director of the Cloud Business Unit of FireEye Inc. He was also the Lead Researcher and VP of Secure DNA and was an Information Technology Consultant for the Office of Regional Economic Integration (OREI) of the Asian Development Bank (ADB).

He is coauthor of the book *Information Security Risk Assessment Toolkit: Practical Assessments through Data Collection and Data Analysis* from Syngress. He has presented in various security and academic conferences and organizations around the world, including Blackhat, Defcon, Shakacon, INFORMS, INFRAGARD, ISSA, and ISACA. He has a number of published papers to his name in various peer-reviewed journals and is also an alumni member of the Honeynet Project.

He has a Master of Liberal Arts Degree (ALM) in Extension Studies (conc. Information Management) from Harvard University and a Master of Science (MS) degree in Information Technology from Ateneo de Manila University. He holds several certifications, including Certified Information Systems Security Professional (CISSP), Certified Information Systems Auditor (CISA), and Certified in Risk and Information Systems Control (CRISC).

Robert McPherson leads a team of data scientists for a Fortune 100 Insurance and Financial Service company in the United States. He has 14 years of experience as a leader of research and analytics teams, specializing in predictive modeling, simulations, econometric analysis, and applied statistics. Robert works with a team of researchers who utilize simulation and big data methods to model the impact of catastrophes on millions of insurance policies…simulating up to 100,000 years of hurricanes, earthquakes, and wildfires, as well as severe winter and summer storms, on more than 2 trillion dollars worth of insured property value. He has used predictive modeling and advanced statistical methods to develop automated outlier detection methods, build automated underwriting models, perform product and customer segmentation analysis, and design competitor war game simulations. Robert has a master's degree in Information Management from the Harvard University Extension.

I. Miyamoto is a computer investigator in a government agency with over 16 years of computer investigative and forensics experience, and 12 years of intelligence analysis experience. I. Miyamoto is in the process of completing a PhD in Systems Engineering and possesses the following degrees: BS in Software Engineering, MA in National Security and Strategic Studies, MS in Strategic Intelligence, and EdD in Education.

Jason L. Martin is Vice President of Cloud Business for FireEye Inc., the global leader in advanced threat-detection technology. Prior to joining FireEye, Jason was the President and CEO of Secure DNA (acquired by FireEye), a company that provided innovative security products and solutions to companies throughout Asia-Pacific and the U.S. Mainland. Customers included Fortune 1000 companies, global government agencies, state and local governments, and private organizations of all sizes. He has over 15 years of experience in Information Security, is a published author and speaker, and is the cofounder of the Shakacon Security Conference.

Acknowledgments

First and foremost, I would like to thank my coauthors, Robert McPherson and I. Miyamoto for all their support before, during, and after the writing of this book. I would like to thank my boss and friend, Jason Martin, for all his guidance and wisdom. I would also like to thank Howard VandeVaarst for all his support and encouragement. Finally, a special thanks to all the guys in Zvelo for welcoming me into their family. Mahalo.

Ryan

I would like to thank Ryan Talabis for inviting me to participate in this project, while at a pizza party at Harvard University. I would like to thank I. Miyamoto for keeping me on track, and offering valuable feedback. Also, I found the technical expertise and editing advice of Pavan Kristipati, and D. Kaye to be very helpful, and I am very grateful to them for their assistance.

Robert

I owe great thanks to Ryan and Bob for their unconditional support and for providing me with the opportunity to participate in this project. Special thanks should be given to our technical reviewer who "went above and beyond" to assist us in improving our work, and the Elsevier Team for their support and patience.

I. Miyamoto

The authors would like to thank James Ochmann and D. Kaye for their help preparing the manuscript.

Analytics Defined

INTRODUCTION TO SECURITY ANALYTICS

The topic of analysis is very broad, as it can include practically any means of gaining insight from data. Even simply looking at data to gain a high-level understanding of it is a form of analysis. When we refer to analytics in this book, however, we are generally implying the use of methods, tools, or algorithms beyond merely looking at the data. While an analyst should always look at the data as a first step, analytics generally involves more than this. The number of analytical methods that can be applied to data is quite broad: they include all types of data visualization tools, statistical algorithms, querying tools, spreadsheet software, special purpose software, and much more. As you can see, the methods are quite broad, so we cannot possibly cover them all.

For the purposes of this book, we will focus on the methods that are particularly useful for discovering security breaches and attacks, which can be implemented with either for free or using commonly available software. Since attackers are constantly creating new methods to attack and compromise systems, security analysts need a multitude of tools to creatively address this problem. Among tools available, we will examine analytical programming languages that enable analysts to create custom analytical procedures and applications. The concepts in this chapter introduce the frameworks useful for security analysis, along with methods and tools that will be covered in greater detail in the remainder of the book.

CONCEPTS AND TECHNIQUES IN ANALYTICS

Analytics integrates concepts and techniques from many different fields, such as statistics, computer science, visualization, and research operations. Any concept or technique allowing you to identify patterns and insights from data could be considered analytics, so the breadth of this field is quite extensive. In this section, high-level descriptions of some of the concepts and techniques you will encounter in this book will be covered. We will provide more detailed descriptions in subsequent chapters with the security scenarios.

General Statistics

Even simple statistical techniques are helpful in providing insights about data. For example, statistical techniques such as extreme values, mean, median, standard deviations, interquartile ranges, and distance formulas are useful in exploring, summarizing, and visualizing data. These techniques, though relatively simple, are a good starting point for exploratory data analysis. They are useful in uncovering interesting trends, outliers, and patterns in the data. After identifying areas of interest, you can further explore the data using advanced techniques.

We wrote this book with the assumption that the reader had a solid understanding of general statistics. A search on the Internet for "statistical techniques" or "statistics analysis" will provide you many resources to refresh your skills. In Chapter 4, we will use some of these general statistical techniques.

Machine Learning

Machine learning is a branch of artificial intelligence dealing with using various algorithms to learn from data. "Learning" in this concept could be applied to being able to predict or classify data based on previous data. For example, in network security, machine learning is used to assist with classifying email as a legitimate or spam. In Chapters 3 and 6, we will cover techniques related to both Supervised Learning and Unsupervised Learning.

Supervised Learning

Supervised learning provides you with a powerful tool to classify and process data using machine language. With supervised learning you use labeled data, which is a data set that has been classified, to infer a learning algorithm. The data set is used as the basis for predicting the classification of other unlabeled data through the use of machine learning algorithms. In Chapter 5, we will be covering two important techniques in supervised learning:

- Linear Regression, and
- Classification Techniques.

Linear Regression

Linear regression is a supervised learning technique typically used in predicting, forecasting, and finding relationships between quantitative data. It is one of the earliest learning techniques, which is still widely used. For example, this technique can be applied to examine if there was a relationship between a company's advertising budget and its sales. You could also use it to determine if there is a linear relationship between a particular radiation therapy and tumor sizes.

Classification Techniques

The classification techniques that will be discussed in this section are those focused on predicting a qualitative response by analyzing data and recognizing patterns. For example, this type of technique is used to classify whether or not a credit card transaction is fraudulent. There are many different classification techniques or classifiers, but some of the widely used ones include:

- Logistic regression,
- Linear discriminant analysis,
- K-nearest neighbors,
- Trees,
- Neural Networks, and
- Support Vector Machines.

Unsupervised Learning

Unsupervised learning is the opposite of supervised learning, where unlabeled data is used because a training set does not exist. None of the data can be presorted or preclassified beforehand, so the machine learning algorithm is more complex and the processing is time intensive. With unsupervised learning, the machine learning algorithm classifies a data set by discovering a structure through common elements in the data. Two popular unsupervised learning techniques are Clustering and Principal Components Analysis. In Chapter 6, we will demonstrate the Clustering technique.

Clustering

Clustering or cluster analysis is a type of Unsupervised Learning technique used to find commonalities between data elements that are otherwise unlabeled and uncategorized. The goal of clustering is to find distinct groups or "clusters" within a data set. Using a machine language algorithm, the tool creates groups where items in a similar group will, in general, have similar characteristics to each other. A few of the popular clustering techniques include:

- K-Means Clustering, and
- Hierarchical Clustering.

Principal Components Analysis

Principal components analysis is an Unsupervised Learning technique summarizing a large set of variables and reducing it into a smaller representative variables, called "principal components." The objective of this type of analysis is to identify patterns in data and express their similarities and differences through their correlations.

Simulations

A computer simulation (or "sim") is an attempt to model a real-life or hypothetical situation on a computer so that it can be studied to see how the system works. Simulations can be used for optimization and "what if" analysis to study various scenarios. There are two types of simulations:

- System Dynamics
- Discrete Event Simulations

In Chapter 4, we will be dealing specifically with Discrete Event Simulations, which simulates an operation as a discrete sequence of events in time.

Text Mining

Text mining is based on a variety of advance techniques stemming from statistics, machine learning and linguistics. Text mining utilizes interdisciplinary techniques to find patterns and trends in "unstructured data," and is more commonly attributed but not limited to textual information. The goal of text mining is to be able to process large textual data to extract "high quality" information, which will be helpful for providing insights into the specific scenario to which the text mining is being applied. Text mining has a large number of uses to include text clustering, concept extraction, sentiment analysis, and summarization. We will be covering text mining techniques in Chapter 6.

Knowledge Engineering

Knowledge engineering is the discipline of integrating human knowledge and/or decision making into computer systems. Typically, these are used to recreate abilities and decision-making process to allow computer systems to solve complex problems that otherwise would only be possible through human expertise. It is widely used in expert systems, artificial intelligence, and decision support systems. We touch upon knowledge engineering techniques in Chapter 3.

DATA FOR SECURITY ANALYTICS

Much of the challenge in performing security analytics stems from the irregular data that the analyst must handle. There is no single standard data format or set of data definitions pertaining to data produced by computer systems and networks. For example, each server software package produces its own log file format. Additionally, these formats can generally be customized by users, which adds to the difficulty of building standard software tools for analyzing the data.

Another factor further complicating the analysis is that log files and other source data are usually produced in plain text format, rather than being organized into tables or columns. This can make it difficult or even impossible to import the data directly into familiar analytical tools, such as Microsoft Excel.

Additionally, security-related data is increasingly becoming too large to analyze with standard tools and methods. Large organizations may have multiple large data centers with an ever-growing collection of servers that are together by sprawling networks. All of this generates a huge volume of log files, which takes us into the realm of Big Data.

Big Data

Over the years, businesses have increased the amount of data they collect. They are now at the point where maintaining large data repositories is part of their business model—which is where the buzzword phrase "big data" emerges.

In some industries, increases in government regulation caused business to collect more data, while in other industries shifts in business practices (online environment or the use of new technologies) enabled businesses to accumulate and store more data. However, much of the data the businesses acquired were unstructured and in many different formats, so it was difficult to convert this data into business intelligence for use in decision making. This all changed when data analytics entered into the picture.

One of the first uses of data analytics was to convert a customer's clicks into business intelligence so that advertisements and products could be tailored to the customer. In this example, data analytics integrated traditional data collection with behavioral analysis (what customers browsed) and predictive analysis (suggestions of products or websites to influence a customer) so that businesses could increase sales and provide a better online experience. Early on, the financial sector also used data analytics to detect credit card fraud by examining a customer's spending patterns and predicting fraudulent transactions based on anomalies and other algorithms.

The driving force behind the "hype" for big data is the need for businesses to have intelligence to make business decisions. Innovative technology is not the primary reason for the growth of the big data industry—in fact, many of the technologies used in data analysis, such as parallel and distributed processing, and analytics software and tools, were already available. Changes in business practices (e.g., a shift to the cloud) and the application of techniques from other fields (engineering, uncertainty analysis, behavioral science, etc.) are what is driving the growth of data analytics. This emerging area created a new industry with experts (data scientists), who are able to examine and configure the different types of data into usable business intelligence.

Many of the same analytical methods can be applied to security. These methods can be used to uncover relationships within data produced by servers and networks to reveal intrusions, denial of service attacks, attempts to install malware, or even fraudulent activity.

Security analysis can range from simple observation by querying or visualizing the data, to applying sophisticated artificial intelligence applications. It can involve the use of simple spreadsheets on small samples of data, to applying big data, parallel-computing technologies to store, process and analyze terabytes, or even petabytes of data.

In the chapters that follow, we hope to provide you with a foundation of security analytics, so that you can further explore other applications. We will include methods ranging from the simple to the complex, to meet the needs of a variety of analysts and organizations, both big and small.

Some analysis may only involve relatively small data sets, such as the instance in which a server has low traffic and only produces a single log file. However, data size can quickly increase, along with the computational power required for analysis when multiple servers are involved.

Two technologies, Hadoop and MapReduce, are being used in tandem to perform analysis using parallel computing. Both are free, open source software, and are maintained by the Apache Foundation ("Welcome to The Apache Software Foundation!," 2013).

Hadoop is a distributed file system that enables large data sets to be split up and stored on many different computers. The Hadoop software manages activities, such as linking the files together and maintaining fault tolerance, "behind-the-scenes." MapReduce is a technology running on top of the Hadoop distributed file system, and does the "heavy lifting" number crunching and data aggregations.

Hadoop and MapReduce have greatly reduced the expense involved in processing and analyzing big data. Users now have the power of a traditional data warehouse at a fraction of the cost through the use of open-source software and off-the-shelf hardware components. In Chapter 3, we will use an implementation of Hadoop and MapReduce that is provided by Cloudera. These technologies are also available in cloud computing environments, such as the Elastic MapReduce service offered by Amazon Web Services ("Amazon Web Services, Cloud Computing: Compute, Storage, Database," 2013). Cloud computing solutions offer flexibility, scalability, and pay-as-you-go affordability. While the field of big data is broad and ever expanding, we will narrow our focus to Hadoop and MapReduce due to their ubiquity and availability.

ANALYTICS IN EVERYDAY LIFE

Analytics in Security

The use of analytics is fairly widespread in our world today. From banking to retail, it exists in one form of the other. But what about security? Below are some examples of how analytics techniques used in other fields can be applied in the field of information security.

Analytics, Incident Response, and Intrusion Detection

Incident response is one of the core areas of a successful security program. Good incident response capabilities allow organizations to contain incidents, and eradicate and recover from the effects of an incident to their information resources.

But to effectively eradicate and recover from a security incident, an incident responder needs to be able to identify the root cause of an incident. For example, let's say your organization's corporate website got hacked. The organization can simply restore the site using backups but without knowing the root cause, you would neither know the vulnerability causing the hack nor would you know what to fix so that the website does not get hacked again. You also might not know the full extent of the damage done, or what information may have been stolen.

How does an incident responder know what to fix? First, the responder has to be able to trace the activities attributed to the intruder. These can be found in various data sources such as logs, alerts, traffic captures, and attacker artifacts. In most cases, a responder will start off with logs, as they can help with finding activities that can be traced back to the intruder. By tracing the activities of the intruder, an incident responder is able to create a history of the attack, thereby detect and identify possible "points of entry" of the intrusion.

What are these logs and how do we obtain them? This really depends on the type of intrusion to which you are responding. For example, in web compromises an incident responder will typically look at web server logs, but remember that this is not always the case. Some attack vectors show up in completely different data sources, which is why reviewing different data sources is important.

So now, what has analytics got to do with incident response and intrusion detection? Analytics techniques can help us to solve incident response and intrusion detection challenges. Next, we will discuss how analytics is applicable to security.

Large and Diverse Data

One of the main challenges in incident response is the sheer amount of data to review. Even reviewing the logs from a busy web server for one day can be a challenge. What if a responder has to review several years of logs? Aside from this, what if a responder had to review multiple server logs during the same time period? The data an incident responder has to sift through would be immense—potentially millions of lines of log information!

This is where analytics and big data techniques come into play. Using big data techniques, an incident responder will be able to combine many data sources with different structures together. Once that is completed, analytics techniques such as fuzzy searches, outlier detection, and time aggregations can be utilized to "crunch" the data into more manageable data sets so responders can focus their investigations on a smaller, more relevant subset of the data.

Aside from logs, analytics techniques, such as text analysis, which can be used to mine information from unstructured data sources, may also be useful. For example, these techniques can be used to analyze security events from free-form text data such as service desk calls. This type of analysis could potentially provide insight into your organization, such as what are the common security problems, or even find security issues or incidents previously unknown.

Unknown Unknowns

A fairly common way to investigate or detect intrusions is by using signatures or patterns. This means that for each attack, an incident responder would try to find the attack by looking for patterns matching the attack. For example, for an SQL injection attack, an incident responder will probably look for SQL statements in the logs. Basically, the responder already knows what he/she is looking for or "Known Unknowns." This approach usually works, it does not cover "Unknown Unknowns."

Unknown Unknowns are attacks that the incident responder has no knowledge of. This could be a zero-day attack or just something that the incident responder, or the investigative tool being utilized, is unfamiliar with or does not address. Typically, signature-based approaches are weak in detecting these types of attacks. Finding Unknown Unknowns are more in the realm of anomaly detection. For example, finding unusual spikes in traffic or outliers by using cluster analysis are good examples of analytics techniques that could potentially find incidents, which would otherwise have been missed by traditional means. It also helps in focusing the investigation to relevant areas, especially if there is a lot of data to sift through.

Simulations and Security Processes

An information security professional makes many decisions that affecting the security of an organization's information systems and resources. These decisions are oftentimes based on a security professional's expertise and experience. However, sometimes it is difficult to make decisions because a security professional may lack of expertise or experience in a particular area. While there may be research studies available, more often than not, it does not apply to the context and situation of the organization.

In this situation, an alternative approach is to use simulations. As stated in the previous section, simulations are computer models of real-life or hypothetical situations. Simulations are used to study how a system works. Think of how the military creates simulations for bombing raids. Simulations help the Air Force to make decisions as to how many planes should be used, to estimate potential losses, and to implement the raids in different scenarios or conditions. Simulations can be implemented in the same way for information security. It might not be as exciting as with military applications, but it can be a powerful tool to study information security scenarios and to help security professionals make informed decisions.

Try Before You Buy

The best way to explore the possibilities of simulations in security is through examples. For example, if a security analyst wanted to see the effect of a virus or malware infection in an organization, how would the security analyst go about doing this? Obviously, the simplest and most accurate solution is to infect the network with live malware! But, of course, we cannot do that. This is where simulations come in. By doing some creative computer modeling, you can potentially create a close approximation of how malware would spread in your organization's information systems.

The same concept can be applied to other scenarios. You can model hacker attacks and couple them with vulnerability results to show their potential effect to your network. This is somewhat akin to creating a virtual simulated penetration test.

Simulation-Based Decisions

Aside from studying scenarios, simulations can be used to assist with making decisions based on the simulated scenarios. For example, perhaps you want to acquire technologies, such as data loss prevention and full disk encryption to prevent data loss. You could use simulations in this context to see the effect of a scenario before it actually happens. Subsequently, the impact of these scenarios can be leveraged to validate or reject your decision-making process.

Access Analytics

Logical access controls are a first line of defense for computer information systems. These are tools used to identify, authorize and maintain accountability regarding access to an organization's computer resources. Unfortunately, in cases where the credentials of users of an organization are compromised, access controls are obviously a moot-point. Unless you are using a strong means of authentication, such as two-factor, attackers can login into the organization's system using valid credentials.

So, how does a security analyst identify these valid, yet unauthorized access attempts? While it is difficult to identify them with certainty, it is possible to identify events, which do not conform to the usual access behavior. This is very similar to how credit card providers identify unusual transactions based on previous spending behaviors. With user access, it is the exact same thing. Typically, users in an organization will have regular patterns of accessing computer systems and anything outside that behavior can be flagged as anomalous.

One important area to which this technique can be applied is with virtual private network (VPN) access. Depending on a user profile, a VPN access allows for a remote connection to internal systems. If user credentials with high privileges are compromised, then the attacker has a greater potential for gaining higher access and for causing greater damages. An important way to ensure this type of access is not abused is by performing an access review. For example, if a user account concurrently logs in from two different geographical locations, a red flag should be triggered. Another example would be to check for unusual access and timing patterns, such as multiple sign-in and sign-off in a short-time period or unusual time references (e.g., early morning hours cross-correlated with the IP address' time zone).

Reviewing this data is not trivial—even looking through a week of user access logs is a significant task. Besides, how do you efficiently correlate different access events? This is where analytics comes into play.

The Human Element

A lot of the logic to detect unusual access events are made just by using common sense. But in some cases, detecting the anomalous event depends on a security analyst's expertise and years of experience. For example, identifying the access behavior of an advanced persistent threat actor is highly specialized, thereby making it difficult for most analysts to find the time and resources to manually perform the analysis.

This is where knowledge engineering comes into play. Knowledge engineering, as discussed in the previous section, is a discipline integrating human expertise into computer systems. Basically, it is meant to automate or at least assist in manual decision making. If one can recreate the logic in identifying anomalous access events through knowledge engineering, the process of identifying them would be simpler, faster and can potentially be automated. For example, if one can just export various access logs, run them through an expert system program, which could be as simple as a script that utilizes conditional matching and rules, then a security analyst may be able to leverage this system to efficiently identify potential compromises and abuses to a company's information systems and resources.

Categorization and Classification in Vulnerability Management

Vulnerabilities are the bane of any organization. Vulnerabilities are weaknesses or flaws that increases the risk of attackers being able to compromise an information system.

Vulnerability Management, on the other hand, is the process to identify, classify, remediate and mitigate vulnerabilities. This is one of the core security processes in any organization. But as many security professionals know, setting up the process may be easy but managing and obtaining value out of the process is another matter.

Currently, networks are getting larger and larger. Systems can now be deployed so easily that there are a lot more systems crammed in our network. With all the vulnerability scanners out there, we have a wealth of vulnerability data that we can work with.

But of course, this comes at a price, because the more data we collect, the more confusing the output becomes. It is common to see security professionals wading through spreadsheets with hundreds of thousands of rows of vulnerability results. This can be overwhelming, and more often than not, the value of this data is often watered down because security professionals do not have the tools or techniques to effectively leverage this data to gain insights about their organization's vulnerabilities and risk.

Birds Eye View

A vulnerability scanner could spew out thousands and thousands of results. It is fairly easy to "drown" in the results by just going through them one by one. However, from a strategic and enterprise standpoint, it may not be the best way to manage vulnerabilities. By using analytics techniques such as clustering and visualization, organizations may be able to identify areas of "hot spots," thereby utilize resources more effectively and address vulnerabilities more systematically.

Predicting Compromises

Another potentially interesting application in vulnerability management is to predict future compromises based on previous compromises. For example, if a web server was hacked and the cause was unknown, analytics techniques such as machine learning could be used to "profile" the compromised server and to check if there are other similar servers in your organizations that have the same profile. Servers with similar profiles would most likely be at risk of similar compromises and should be proactively protected.

Prioritization and Ranking

To have an effective vulnerability management process, it is important for organizations to understand not only the vulnerabilities itself but also the interplay between other external data, such as exploit availability and the potential impact to the assets themselves. This is basic risk management in which techniques such as decision trees, text analysis and various correlation techniques would help in combining all the data and in forming insights based on the correlations.

SECURITY ANALYTICS PROCESS

Our goal is to provide you with an overview of the Security Analytics Process. Figure 1.1 provides a conceptual framework of how we envision the process. Chapters 2 through 6 demonstrate the first two steps of the process by showing you how to select your data and to use security analytics. Our focus with this book is to provide you with the tools for the first two steps in the process. In Chapter 7, we provide you with an overview of security intelligence and how it can be used to improve your organization's response posture.

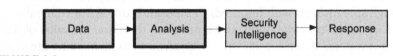

FIGURE 1.1

REFERENCES

Amazon, 2013 Amazon Web Services, Cloud Computing: Compute, Storage, Database. (2013). Retrieved September 16, 2013, from http://aws.amazon.com/.

Apache Software, 2013 Welcome to the Apache Software Foundation! (September 2013). Retrieved September 16, 2013, from http://apache.org/.

Primer on Analytical Software and Tools

INTRODUCTION

In this chapter, we will introduce some freely available, open source software and programming languages that are useful for security analytics. The reader should gain at least some familiarity with these, to follow the examples in subsequent chapters in this book.

There are many high-end, and high-priced vendor supplied software packages that are designed for specific security analysis tasks, such as proprietary text mining software, and intrusion detection packages. Since many analysts may not have access to these packages without having a sizable budget, our purpose is to introduce tools and methods that are readily available, regardless of budget size.

Additionally, many proprietary vendor packages restrict the user to a set of methods that are predefined in a graphical user interface (GUI). A GUI can make software easier to use, but it can also limit the user to only being able to access certain analytical methods. While we will discuss some open source graphical interfaces that may be useful in exploring some data sets, many of our analytical methods will require some coding to implement. Learning how to write analytical methods in code is worthwhile, since this offers the maximum flexibility in discovering new attack vectors, such as those common in zero day attacks.

By the end of the chapter, readers will be introduced to a range of powerful analytical tools, most of which are freely available to download from the Internet. The details on how to use these tools will come in the chapters that follow.

STATISTICAL PROGRAMMING

The discovery of attackers and their methods requires the ability to spot patterns in large and complex data sets, such as server logs. Unfortunately, the larger and more complex a data set becomes, we humans find ourselves less able to discern relevant patterns. Statistical methods and tools provide a lens to help us spot key relationships within the data.

Many people cringe at the very mention of statistics. However, anyone who has ever counted, summed, averaged, or compared numbers has been doing statistical analysis—basic analysis, but analysis no less. These simpler kinds of statistics, referred to as descriptive statistics, are actually the most important starting point to any analysis. As simple and easy to understand as descriptive statistics are, they are the best way of understanding the data you are dealing with, and often reveal a lot of interesting patterns on their own. For these reasons, the calculation and analysis of descriptive statistics should always be one of the first steps in analyzing your data.

Of course, there are more complex statistical tools that we will find very useful in doing analysis. Fortunately, these statistical methods are packaged up within software, so that you do not have to be too concerned with the inner workings under the hood. Using these tools generally only involves calling up a function in your code, or in some cases, clicking on a menu item in a user interface. More advanced statistical methods include some of those mentioned previously, such as clustering, correlation, regression, and a host of machine learning and predictive modeling tools.

There are many software tools and programming languages that are capable of performing statistical analysis. Examples include R, Python, Arena, Mahout, Stata, SAS, VB/VBA, and SQL. Rather than risk covering too many of them, we will, for the most part, focus on those that are the most widely used, and which can be downloaded and used at no cost. We will focus on R, HiveQL, and Python for most of our examples. We will also use Apache Mahout for statistical analysis on very large data sets, and Arena for simulation modeling. (While the Arena software package does have a cost, a free trial version is available to download.) By far, the most popular open source statistical programming language is R. In fact, it is now in such widespread use worldwide, and has so many analytical packages available, that this language is being called the "lingua franca of statistics" by a growing number of data analysts across many disciplines (Vance, 1996). One of the features which makes R so powerful for statistical analysis, is that it is capable of manipulating and performing operations on entire matrices at a time, rather than being limited to arrays or vectors. R often requires fewer lines of code to perform statistical analysis than many other alternative languages.

R offers a rich data analysis and programming environment that includes thousands of freely available add-on packages for data importing, cleansing, transforming, visualizing, mining, and analyzing. There are even packages for adding graphical interfaces which make data exploration faster, by minimizing the amount of code that must be written. Examples of interfaces for R include the Rattle, and R Commander packages.

INTRODUCTION TO DATABASES AND BIG DATA TECHNIQUES

The phrase, "big data," has become so overused in so many contexts, that it can be difficult to discern what it really means. While there is no single definition, a common explanation is that data qualifies as big data if it has characteristics pertaining to at least one of the three V's: volume, velocity, and variability. Volume refers to the size of the data, usually measured in the number of rows, or in the number of bytes. There is no specified size that qualifies data as being big, but data sets containing billions of rows, or multiple terabytes are common. As discussed in Chapter 1, big data generally utilizes parallel computing to process such high volumes.

Hadoop and MapReduce software together provide a very popular platform for big data work. Hadoop is a distributed file system developed at Google, and enables large data sets to be spread out among many computers that work together simultaneously. MapReduce software enables data aggregation routines to be run on top of the Hadoop distributed file system.

To work with the server log examples provided in Chapter 6, you will need to install some big data software on a virtual machine on your computer. The virtual machine allows you to run a Linux operating system on your Windows or Apple computer. You need to have a working Hive environment, on top of a Hadoop file system, loaded with MapReduce. Fortunately, these elements are preinstalled in the free Cloudera QuickStart VM, from http://www.cloudera.com. As of this writing, this software package can be downloaded from http://www.cloudera.com/content/cloudera-content/cloudera-docs/DemoVMs/Cloudera-QuickStart-VM/cloudera_quickstart_vm.html. Additionally, we will do some analysis with Mahout and R, so it will be helpful to have these loaded onto your virtual machine as well.

To install R on your virtual machine, you will need to use some Unix commands from a terminal window. Also referred to as a shell, open a terminal window by selecting Applications>System Tools>Terminal from the menu bar at the top of the CentOS desktop. You will need to make sure you have an internet connection. By way of background, if you have never used a Unix command line before, you will see a dollar-sign symbol, which customarily indicates the place after which you can type your commands. Examples are shown in the lines below. You should not type the dollar signs into your commands yourself, as these are simply shown to represent the command prompt. From the shell prompt, type the following commands to install R.

```
$   rpm -ivh http://mirror.chpc.utah.edu/pub/epel/5/x86_64/
epel-release-5-4.noarch.rpm
$   sudo yum install R
```

To install Mahout, type the following command.

```
$   sudo yum install mahout
```

The word, sudo, in the above commands indicates that you are entering super user mode. This allows you to install software, and to access root level directories in your file system. The sudo command will also cause you to be prompted to enter a password as well, after you hit the enter key. When you first install your Cloudera virtual machine, your default username and password will be "admin." The yum command starts the package installer used by the CentOS operating system.

INTRODUCTION TO R

When you want to combine and automate data preparation, analysis, visualization, and presentation all in one environment, R is a very useful language. There are thousands of packages available to perform all manner of tasks related to data, and new ones are continuously being developed and released. You can find R software, packages, and documentation in the Comprehensive R Archive Network (CRAN). This online repository also serves as the main Website for the R community. It is located at www.cran.r-project.org. At this Website, you will find instructions for downloading and installing R, as well as documentation. This is also the best place to search for packages that you may wish to download. While R comes with a large amount of base packages, there are many add-on packages that can greatly extend R's capabilities.

R is more than a scripting language to perform statistical calculations. It is a full featured, object oriented programming language. This makes R a very flexible and powerful tool for data analysts. The R language can be used for many diverse and helpful purposes, including extracting, cleansing, and transforming data, producing visualizations, performing analysis, and publishing attractive finished documents and presentations. Although all this flexibility may appear to come at the cost of a somewhat steep learning curve, the power it affords the analyst in uncovering hidden insights is worth the effort.

Learning the R programming language is beyond the scope of this book. It is assumed that the reader already knows some R, or is willing to invest some time into learning it. However, we will provide some introductory material here, so that readers who have at least some programming experience in other languages, will be able to read and follow along with some of the code examples in this book. We also suggest freely available resources to those who want to study R in greater depth.

There are many ways to learn R—many of them for no cost. A course is a very good way, for those who are academically inclined. There are numerous Massive Open Online Courses available focusing on R, which are offered free of charge. Coursera (www.coursera.com) is one such resource. There are also freely available texts and manuals available for downloading from the CRAN R Website as well (www.cran.r-project.org). One such popular text is a downloadable manual called, "An Introduction to R" (Cran.r-project.org, 2014). There are also numerous videos available, including a series made available by Google called, "Series of Tutorials for Developers in R." An internet search on terms such as "R tutorial" will produce many other resources as well. In fact, this may be the best way to locate tutorials, since new ones are continually coming out, due to the growing popularity of the language.

Similar to Python, R is an interpreted language, as opposed to a compiled language. This means that you can type a line of R code at the R command line, and see the result immediately upon pressing the enter key. Unlike languages like C or Java, you do not need to compile your code first before running it. This allows you to easily experiment as you write your code—you can test your code as you build it, one line at a time.

For example, if you type 2+2 at the command prompt in R, and then hit enter, a line of output will appear below where you typed, showing the answer, 4. The command prompt is indicated by the symbol, ">". The square brackets containing the number "1" is called an index value, and indicates that there is only one item in this answer.

```
>  2+2
[1]  4
```

Much of the work done in R is accomplished by functions that are stored in packages. If you are familiar with the Java language, functions may be thought of as analogous to methods in Java. In fact, you may notice that R looks a little like Java in the way that parentheses and brackets are used. In addition, the operators are also similar. However, there are significant differences. For example, the data types are quite different, and the dot is not used as a separator of object names in R as they are used in Java.

The data types in R are as follows.

- vectors
- matrices
- arrays

- data frames
- lists
- factors

(Kabacoff, 2012b)

Many of the operators in R should be familiar to users of a popular spreadsheet software. The following are common operators.

Assignment Operators

= assignment left
<- assignment left
-> assignment right

Arithmetic Operators

+ plus
– minus
/ divide
* multiply
%% modulus
%/% integer division
^ or ** exponentiation

Logical Operators

< less than
> greater than
== equality
!= inequality
<= less than or equal to
>= greater than or equal to
| or
& and
TRUE is true
FALSE is false

(Kabacoff, 2012a)

There are key differences. For example, note that the assignment operator can be expressed in two ways: the equal sign, which is similar to many other languages, and the less than and dash symbols, which when combined as in <-, look like an arrow. The arrow operator can also point the other direction, as in ->, although this is rarely used. The arrow symbol works the same way as the equal sign. However, the equal sign can only assign a value to a name appearing to the left of it, and it cannot assign a value to the right, as the arrow symbol can. It is really just a matter of preference as to which one you choose to use. In this book, we will primarily use the equal sign, since that is familiar to programmers of most of the popular modern languages.

The use of dots in names in R deserves some explanation, since this often confuses newcomers to R from object oriented languages such as C and Java. It is fairly common to see examples of R code that uses a dot within a variable name. In R, a dot in a name simply serves as a visual separator to make names easier to read. However, in Java a dot in a name like MyClass.myMethod() indicates a method called "myMethod" contained within a class called "MyClass."

Most of the work in R is done using functions. Programming in R often requires a lot of referencing of help screens to learn how to use the many functions that are available. Even very experienced R programmers have to refer to help screens, as new functions continually become available. One of the most important R skills to learn, then, is to navigate and use the R help documentation. There are a couple ways to look up the help documentation for a function. From the R command line, you can type help(), and put the function name within the parentheses. Or, you can type a question mark in front of the function name, such as ?lm, which in this case will bring up the help documentation and examples for the "linear model" function, lm().

Common R Functions

While there are thousands of R functions available in the many R packages that can be downloaded from the CRAN R repository, there are few essential functions you will find yourself using time and again. Fortunately, most of these functions are contained in the base package when you download the R language.

For example, the function, c(), is a function to concatenate. You can group objects, such as variables, together in a single object and save the result as a new variable name.

```
a = 1
b = 2
c = 3
myList = c(a, b, c)
```

INTRODUCTION TO PYTHON

Python is a relatively easy to learn, while being a powerful programming language. The syntax allows programmers to create programs in fewer lines than it would be possible in other languages. It also features a fairly large, comprehensive library, and third-party tools. It has interpreters for multiple operating systems. So, if you are using Windows, a Mac or a Linux based machine, you should be able to access and use Python. Finally, Python is free and since it is open-source, your code and applications may be freely distributed.

Python is an interpreted language. This means you do not have to compile it as you would other more traditional languages, like C or C++. Python is geared for rapid development, saving you considerable time in program development. As such, it is perfect for simple automation tasks, such as those we have planned for in our scenario in Chapter 5. Aside from this, the interpreter can also be used interactively, providing an interface for easy experimentation.

A more detailed primer is provided in the chapter regarding Access Control Analytics, and additional discussions and resources regarding Python are made available there.

INTRODUCTION TO SIMULATION SOFTWARE

One of the tools that we will be using in the Simulations Chapter is Arena. Arena is a powerful modeling and simulation software allowing a user to model and run simulation experiments. The commercial version of Arena is available for purchase from Rockwell Automation but a fully functioning perpetual evaluation version is available for study (http://www.arenasimulation.com/Tools_Resources_Download_Arena.aspx).

Arena is a Windows desktop application and can be installed in systems running Windows. After installing Arena and starting the program, you will see the main Arena window consisting of three main regions:

- The Project bar typically found in the left had side of the main window contains three tabs, the Basic process, Report and Navigate Panel. This bar is contains the various Arena modules that are used to build a simulation model. We will discuss more about what "Arena modules" are in the latter part of this section.
- The Model window flowchart view typically located on the right had side of the main window makes up the largest part of the screen real estate. This is your workspace where you create your model. The model is graphically created in the form of flowcharts, images, animations and other drawn elements.
- The Model window spreadsheet view typically located at the bottom part of the flowchart view presents all the data associated with the model.

A whole chapter is dedicated to making simulations, so at this point, we will provide a high level overview of creating simulations in Arena. There are three main steps in making a simulation in Arena:

1. Design and create the model,
2. Add data and parameters to the model,
3. Run the simulation, and
4. Analyze the simulation.

Designing and Creating the Model

Before creating a model, you must first create a "conceptual model" of the scenario you would like to simulate. This could be anything from you just drawing it out in a piece of paper or just thinking about it.

Once you have a conceptual model, the next step is to build the model in the workspace using the various "modules" in Arena. Modules are the building blocks of a model. There are two kinds of modules, the flowchart modules and the data modules.

The Flowchart modules illustrate the logic of your simulation. Some common flowchart modules are Create, Process, Decide, Disposes, Batch, Separate, Assign and Record, which you will find in the "Basic Process" tab in the Project bar. To use these modules, you simply drag the flowchart modules needed into the model and then connect the modules together in the Model window flowchart view.

A bit confused? Don't worry because we have a whole chapter about this. Additionally, this quick start model is provided in the companion site for download. For now, just think that you will basically creating a flowchart of your scenario. If you have used Microsoft Visio, you will be right at home.

Adding Data and Parameters to the Model

After creating the flowchart, the next step to in creating a simulation in Arena is to add data to each of the flowchart modules. Various values can be assigned for each module by double clicking the modules in the model.

Running the Simulation

After the model is complete, all you need to do is to select "Go" from the Run menu or press F5. There are other parameters that you may want to set up before running the simulation such as the replication parameters where you can set the simulation period. But for the purpose of this quick introduction, just running the simulation will suffice.

Analyzing the Simulation

Arena provides you with reports that allow you to analyze the simulation. You can be accessed these reports from the Reports panel in the Project bar. The report provides statistics such as max, min, averages, and resource reports related to the simulation you just ran.

Arena is a very powerful and versatile simulation development tool using a simple method to set up the simulation model and parameters. Aside from being fairly easy to use, it comes with good documentation with the software installation. The documentation can be found in the Help menu under the Arena product manuals. The "Getting Started with Arena" is a fairly good document from which to start learning about Arena.

REFERENCES

Cran.r-project.org, 2014. An Introduction to R (online) Available at http://www.cran.r-project. org/doc/manuals/r-release/R-intro.html (accessed 15.10.2013).

Kabacoff, R., 2012a. Quick-R: Data Management (online) Available at http://www.statmethods. net/management/operators.html (accessed 22.10.2013).

Kabacoff, R., 2012b. Quick-R: Data Types (online) Available at http://www.statmethods.net/ input/datatypes.html (accessed 24.10.2013).

Vance, A., 1996. R, the Software, Finds Fans in Data Analysts (online) Available at http://www. nytimes.com/2009/01/07/technology/business-computing/07program.html?_r=0 (accessed 14.10.2013).

## CHAPTER 3

Analytics and Incident Response

INFORMATION IN THIS CHAPTER:

- Scenarios and Challenges in Intrusions and Incident Identification
- Use of Text Mining and Outlier Detection
- Case Study: Step by step guide how to use statistical programming tools to find Intrusions and Incidents (Case study will be about server log investigation using Hadoop and R)
- Other Applicable Security Areas and Scenarios

INTRODUCTION

Server security is a top concern, as widely publicized data breaches are increasingly in the news. After a data breach occurs, forensic analysis of server logs is necessary to identify vulnerabilities, perform damage assessments, prescribe mitigation measures, and collect evidence. However, the increasing amount of Internet traffic, accompanied by growing numbers of Web servers in data centers, often produces massive collections of server log data, which are difficult to analyze with traditional, nonparallelized methods.

By using the Hadoop, MapReduce, and Hive software stack, you have the ability to simultaneously analyze very large collections of server logs. Hadoop and MapReduce together provide a distributed file structure, and parallel processing framework, while Hive provides the ability to query and analyze data with an SQL-like syntax. R gives you the essential analytical tools that can be used on moderate-sized data sets, or on big data that have been aggregated or filtered down to a more manageable size utilizing Hadoop and MapReduce.

There are commercial tools available to help you with querying log-file data. Some, such as Splunk, are capable of handling big data as well. However, we will be focusing the examples in this chapter on open-source and freely available tools and analytical platforms. By writing your own scripts, you can fully customize your analysis to your situation and can build repeatable processes as well. Open-source tools, such as R, offer thousands of analytical packages to choose from, including very sophisticated and cutting-edge methods that may not be available in commercial toolsets.

Commercial tools can be quite expensive, and not all organizations and departments have the budget for them. However, if you have access to commercial tools, by all means, use them to their fullest advantage. Commercial tools allow for very rapid exploration of your data, utilizing graphical user interfaces, which can make them well worth the cost. Even though scripts are great for reproducibility, which can be a huge advantage when you need to retrace your steps, or rerun your analysis on new data, they do take some time and effort to write. Therefore, it is difficult to beat a good graphical interface for rapid initial searches through your data.

Given that commercial tools and open-source tools each have their advantages, they should be viewed as complementary rather than competing technologies. If you can afford it, why not utilize both? Once you learn how to perform analysis using open-source tools, such as Hadoop, MapReduce, R, and Mahout, you will have a solid foundation for understanding the analytical process on any platform. This will help you in learning other tools, including commercial tools.

In this chapter, we will explore scenarios and examples for using analytical methods to uncover potential security breaches. The methods covered in this section are not intended to be an exhaustive catalog of the possibilities. Rather, we hope they will help you to develop some creative ideas of your own.

SCENARIOS AND CHALLENGES IN INTRUSIONS AND INCIDENT IDENTIFICATION

Perhaps the greatest challenge in identifying intrusion attempts is that "we do not know what we do not know." It is difficult to uncover the unknown-unknowns: new attack patterns that we cannot foresee and which can circumvent existing defenses. Software programs used for preventing intrusions in real time are essential, but they have a significant shortcoming. In general, they only detect known patterns of attack—or, known attack vectors, in security parlance. Real-time intrusion detection and prevention tends to focus on the known-unknowns, rather than the unknown-unknowns.

While deploying real-time intrusion detection and prevention defenses is essential, it is not enough. Analysts need to use creative efforts to uncover new attacks that successfully circumvent existing defenses. It involves analyzing data gathered from systems, such as the log files from servers and network appliances and the drives from personal computing devices.

In this chapter, we will focus on the analysis of data, rather than the gathering of data. There are many good texts and online resources available for ideas on how to gather data. Since most systems already gather much data about network and server traffic, the greater challenge is in knowing what to do with the data, rather than in collecting it. Whether the data source consists of server logs, network data from software such as Wireshark, or from some other sources, the analytical methods are generally the same. For example, regardless of the data source, outlier detection methods are very likely to be useful, in any situation.

Analyzing a Collection of Server Logs with Big Data

In this section, we will examine how to analyze multiple server logs simultaneously, using big data technologies.

Conducting Analysis with Big Data Tools

We will focus on a variety of queries in the Hive Query Language (HiveQL) to assist in performing forensic analysis of Apache server log files. We will also include some analysis with other software tools, such as R and Mahout. Since HiveQL is very similar to basic ANSI SQL, it should be easily grasped by those who are already familiar with querying relational databases.

In fact, most of the queries here can be run with little or only minor modifications on log-file data that have already been parsed and stored in a relational database. If you have a small enough collection of log files, a relational database may be all that you need. However, for large collections of logs, the parallel processing afforded by Hive running on top of Hadoop could turn an otherwise impossible analysis into one that is doable.

The log files used in the examples that follow are in the popular Apache combined format. This code can be easily adapted to other formats as well.

ANALYSIS OF LOG FILES

Although there is no single standard for server log formats, there are, however, a few formats that are relatively common. Examples include log-file formats for Windows Event Logs, IIS logs, firewall logs, VPN access logs, and various UNIX logs for authentication, FTP, SSH, and so on. However, open-source server software from the Apache Foundation is very common and produces log files in a couple formats: common log format and combined log format. Although these formats can be modified by the user, it is fairly common to see these two formats used without modifications. The combined format is the same as the common format, except that two fields are added. These are the referrer and user agent fields. The referrer field indicates the site that the client was referred or linked from. The user agent shows identifying information on the client browser. The server examples in this book will generally use the combined format, although the methods we will examine can be adapted to any format.

Common Log File Fields

- Remote hostname or IP address of the user
- User's remote logname
- The authenticated username
- The date and time that the request was made
- The URL request string sent from the client
- The http status code that was returned by the server to the client
- The size in number of bytes of the document that was transferred from the server to the client

Combined Log File Fields

- Remote hostname or IP address of the user
- User's remote logname
- The authenticated username
- The date and time that the request was made
- The URL request string sent from the client
- The http status code that was returned by the server to the client
- The size in number of bytes of the document that was transferred from the server to the client
- URL of the site that the client was referred from
- Identifying information on the client browser or user agent

Methods

Methods of analysis include the following:

- Perform fuzzy searches for keywords and terms related to known attack vectors, using LIKE operators. These vectors can include injection attacks, directory and path traversal intrusions, cache poisoning, file inclusion or execution, and denial of service attacks.
- Produce time aggregations of Web log variables for trending, such as host activity, requests, status codes, file sizes, and agents.
- Sort, filter, and combine data to identify potential problem sources.
- Create analytical data sets suitable for further analysis with R and Mahout.

Additional Data and Software Needed to Run these Examples

We have included all of the data required to run this analysis in the Web site of supplementary materials for this book. The data consist of Apache, combined format server log files.

Files one through six are from Amazon's sample collection. However, as there are no known or readily apparent security breaches within these files, an additional file has been added to this collection, containing examples of log entries that are typical of known security breach incidents. This additional file is called, "access_log_7." Some of these incidents were found by searching the Internet for sources. Others were added and were derived from a small collection of examples from some actual Web forensic efforts (Talabis, 2013). For security and privacy reasons, no confidential or personal identifiers remain in these log entries.

SQL-like Analysis with Hive

Hive was used for most of the examples, due to the large number of analysts who are familiar with SQL-like syntax, and the flexibility of Hive's built-in functions and operators. Also, since there are so many potential attack vectors, with new ones being created continually, security analyst needs tools to enable ad hoc, customized analysis. SQL-style tools such as Hive and HiveQL fill this need very nicely.

LOADING THE DATA

The first few steps are basic and involve the following: starting hive, setting up the data, creating the main table, and loading it. It is the analysis part that will become a little more interesting. However, we must first deal with the data setup.

Place the log files in a folder that is shared with your virtual machine you are running. Or, you could also place them in a local directory in Amazon's AWS environment. All of the following examples are demonstrated in a Cloudera virtual machine on my own computer. The files should be loaded into a folder called, "Apach-eLogData." We next navigate to the parent folder, which we called "Project1," and start Hive from there by typing "hive" at our Bash shell command line.

```
[cloudera@localhost Project1]$ hive.
Logging initialized using configuration in jar:file:/usr/lib/hive/
lib/hive-common-0.10.0-cdh4.2.0.jar!/hive-log4j.properties
Hive history file=/tmp/cloudera/hive_job_log_cloud-
era_201305061902_843121553.txt
hive>
```

We need to reference the jar file needed for the deserializer, which is used for parsing the server logs. We do this by adding it on the hive command line, as follows:

```
hive> add jar /usr/lib/hive/lib/hive-contrib-0.10.0-cdh4.2.0.jar;
Added /usr/lib/hive/lib/hive-contrib-0.10.0-cdh4.2.0.jar to class path
```

```
Added resource: /usr/lib/hive/lib/hive-contrib-0.10.0-cdh4.2.0.jar
hive>
```

Next, we add a setting that enables column headers to be seen in the output. This provides a reference making the query results a little easier to read, especially for those who may not be very familiar with the Apache log-file format.

```
hive> set hive.cli.print.header=true;
```

In the next step, we create our base table structure and load it with data.

```
hive> CREATE TABLE apachelog (
    > host STRING,
    > identity STRING,
    > user STRING,
    > time STRING,
    > request STRING,
    > status STRING,
    > size STRING,
    > referer STRING,
    > agent STRING)
    > ROW FORMAT SERDE 'org.apache.hadoop.hive.contrib.serde2.
      RegexSerDe'
    > WITH SERDEPROPERTIES (  "input.regex" = "([^ ]*) ([^ ]*)
      ([^ ]*) (-
    > |\\[[^\\]]*\\]) ([^ \"]*|\"[^\"]*\") (-|[0-9]*) (-|[0-9]*)
      (?: ([^
    > \"]*|\"[^\"]*\") ([^ \"]*|\"[^\"]*\"))?", "output.format.
      string" =
    > "%1$s %2$s %3$s %4$s %5$s %6$s %7$s %8$s %9$s"  )
    > STORED AS TEXTFILE;
OK
Time taken: 0.029 seconds
```

Now we have an empty table and are ready to load all seven of the log files. As previously mentioned, the seventh file is one that we created, containing examples of security breaches. The other six were extracted from Amazon's examples.

```
hive> LOAD DATA LOCAL INPATH "ApacheLogData/access*" INTO TABLE
apachelog;
Copying data from file:/mnt/hgfs/BigDataAnalytics/Project1/
ApacheLogData/access*
Copying file: file:/mnt/hgfs/BigDataAnalytics/Project1/
ApacheLogData/access_log_1
Copying file: file:/mnt/hgfs/BigDataAnalytics/Project1/
ApacheLogData/access_log_2
Copying file: file:/mnt/hgfs/BigDataAnalytics/Project1/
ApacheLogData/access_log_3
Copying file: file:/mnt/hgfs/BigDataAnalytics/Project1/
ApacheLogData/access_log_4
Copying file: file:/mnt/hgfs/BigDataAnalytics/Project1/
ApacheLogData/access_log_5
```

```
Copying file: file:/mnt/hgfs/BigDataAnalytics/Project1/
ApacheLogData/access_log_6
Copying file: file:/mnt/hgfs/BigDataAnalytics/Project1/
ApacheLogData/access_log_7
Loading data to table default.apachelog
Table default.apachelog stats: [num_partitions: 0, num_files: 7,
num_rows: 0, total_size: 53239106, raw_data_size: 0]
OK
Time taken: 0.614 seconds
```

For anyone who may be interested in extracting the Amazon example log files directly, we have provided the following instructions. There is more than one way to do this, but here is the way that we did it. Within Amazon's Elastic MapReduce environment, we made a new directory called, "temp." We then copied all of the sample log files that are stored in Amazon's examples S3 bucket to our new temp directory. The examples are kept in a bucket located at "3n://elasticmapreduce/samples/pig-apache/input/."

```
hadoop@domU-12-31-39-00-88-72:~$ hadoop dfs -mkdir temp
hadoop@domU-12-31-39-00-88-72:~$ hadoop dfs -cp 's3n://elasticma-
preduce/samples/pig-apache/input/*' temp
13/04/22 19:17:43 INFO s3native.NativeS3FileSystem: Opening
's3n://elasticmapreduce/samples/pig-apache/input/access_log_1' for
reading
13/04/22 19:17:46 INFO s3native.NativeS3FileSystem: Opening 's3n://
elasticmapreduce/samples/pig-apache/input/access_log_2' for reading
13/04/22 19:17:48 INFO s3native.NativeS3FileSystem: Opening 's3n://
elasticmapreduce/samples/pig-apache/input/access_log_3' for reading
13/04/22 19:17:49 INFO s3native.NativeS3FileSystem: Opening 's3n://
elasticmapreduce/samples/pig-apache/input/access_log_4' for reading
13/04/22 19:17:50 INFO s3native.NativeS3FileSystem: Opening 's3n://
elasticmapreduce/samples/pig-apache/input/access_log_5' for reading
13/04/22 19:17:52 INFO s3native.NativeS3FileSystem: Opening 's3n://
elasticmapreduce/samples/pig-apache/input/access_log_6' for reading
```

We then moved the files from the temp directory to our own S3 bucket for easier access, in the event that we want to retrieve or modify them in the future. Our S3 bucket was named, "Project1E185."

```
hadoop@domU-12-31-39-00-88-72:~$ hadoop dfs -cp temp/* 's3n://
Project1E185/'
13/04/22 19:19:36 INFO s3native.NativeS3FileSystem: Creating new
file 's3n://Project1E185/access_log_1' in S3
13/04/22 19:19:40 INFO s3native.Jets3tNativeFileSystemStore:
s3.putObject Project1E185 access_log_1 8754118
13/04/22 19:19:40 INFO s3native.NativeS3FileSystem: Creating new
file 's3n://Project1E185/access_log_2' in S3
13/04/22 19:19:42 INFO s3native.Jets3tNativeFileSystemStore:
s3.putObject Project1E185 access_log_2 8902171
```

```
13/04/22 19:19:42 INFO s3native.NativeS3FileSystem: Creating new
file 's3n://Project1E185/access_log_3' in S3
13/04/22 19:19:44 INFO s3native.Jets3tNativeFileSystemStore:
s3.putObject Project1E185 access_log_3 8896201
13/04/22 19:19:44 INFO s3native.NativeS3FileSystem: Creating new
file 's3n://Project1E185/access_log_4' in S3
13/04/22 19:19:46 INFO s3native.Jets3tNativeFileSystemStore:
s3.putObject Project1E185 access_log_4 8886636
13/04/22 19:19:46 INFO s3native.NativeS3FileSystem: Creating new
file 's3n://Project1E185/access_log_5' in S3
13/04/22 19:19:48 INFO s3native.Jets3tNativeFileSystemStore:
s3.putObject Project1E185 access_log_5 8902365
13/04/22 19:19:48 INFO s3native.NativeS3FileSystem: Creating new
file 's3n://Project1E185/access_log_6' in S3
13/04/22 19:19:50 INFO s3native.Jets3tNativeFileSystemStore:
s3.putObject Project1E185 access_log_6 8892828
```

We then downloaded these files from our S3 bucket to the shared folder on our computer called, "ApacheLogData." This is so that we can access them from our Cloudera Hadoop installation.

Discovery Process for Specific Attack Vectors

The most direct means of discovering attack attempts within server logs is to find patterns within the "request" field. The request field shows the URL information for the resource or Web page requested by the user of a client browser, or other agent. Many attacks leave revealing fingerprints or signatures behind within this field, through the use of a LIKE operator, using HQL. Or, if more fine-grained control is required for the search, either the REGEXP or RLIKE operator may be used with a regular expression.

You can do these searches with Perl, Java, or any other tool that can handle regular expressions. However, these tools do not scale up to handling large and numerous log files, as can the combined forces of the Hive, MapReduce, and Hadoop software stack. Following are some examples of direct searches and the attacks they are intended to find.

SQL Injection Attack

In an SQL injection attempt, the attacker tries to insert SQL code within a resource request. When this happens, multiple attempts may be made, with error messages occasionally providing clues to available fields within the database. For example, including a nonexistent variable within a "SELECT" statement on certain databases will produce an error stating that the variable does not exist, followed by a listing of available variables. Through trial and error, the attacker may be able to get into the database to retrieve valuable information or to do damage to the system.

The LIKE statement in Hive turns out to be the same syntax that you would be familiar with on most SQL-based, relational databases. In this case, we want to search the request URL string for terms that would be essential to any SQL query: select, from, where, case, if, having, and when. The code below also uses the Hive function, "LOWER()," to ensure that the LIKE operator will recognize the term, whether or not it is capitalized (making it non-case sensitive). It is important to note that Hive's LIKE operator departs from its counterpart as seen in most relational databases because it is case sensitive. Therefore, we use the LOWER() function to ensure that case sensitivity is not an issue for our query.

```
SELECT * FROM apachelog
WHERE LOWER(request) LIKE '% like %'
OR LOWER(request) LIKE '%select %'
OR LOWER(request) LIKE '% from %'
OR LOWER(request) LIKE '% where %'
OR LOWER(request) LIKE '% if %'
OR LOWER(request) LIKE '% having %'
OR LOWER(request) LIKE '% case %'
OR LOWER(request) LIKE '% when %';
```

It is important to note that these are just a few possibilities given for example sake. There are many other possibilities, and attack vectors are always changing. You can use an Internet search engine to search on keywords, such as sqli or "sql injection examples," to search for updated attack information and adjust your queries accordingly. Also, you should investigate how information is stored on your server logs. Unlike the logs in this example, you may find that your log files do not show any spaces between the keywords. URLs cannot show spaces, so they may appear encoded in your log file as either %20 or with a plus sign, as in "+." To catch these cases, you can simply repeat the above lines in the "WHERE" clause, but eliminate the spaces. For example, "% select %" becomes "%select%."

Running this code segment produces the below output.

```
hive> SELECT * FROM apachelog
  > WHERE LOWER(request) LIKE '% like %'
  > OR LOWER(request) LIKE '%select %'
  > OR LOWER(request) LIKE '% from %'
  > OR LOWER(request) LIKE '% where %'
  > OR LOWER(request) LIKE '% if %'
  > OR LOWER(request) LIKE '% having %'
  > OR LOWER(request) LIKE '% case %'
  > OR LOWER(request) LIKE '% when %';
Total MapReduce jobs = 1
Launching Job 1 out of 1
Number of reduce tasks is set to 0 since there's no reduce operator
Starting Job = job_201305061901_0002, Tracking URL = http://local-
host.localdomain:50030/jobdetails.jsp?jobid=job_201305061901_0002
```

```
Kill Command = /usr/lib/hadoop/bin/hadoop job    -kill
job_201305061901_0002
Hadoop job information for Stage-1: number of mappers: 1; number of
reducers: 0
2013-05-06 20:16:31,416 Stage-1 map = 0%,    reduce = 0%
2013-05-06 20:16:39,459 Stage-1 map = 100%,    reduce = 0%,
Cumulative CPU 4.82 sec
2013-05-06 20:16:40,471 Stage-1 map = 100%,    reduce = 100%,
Cumulative CPU 4.82 sec
MapReduce Total cumulative CPU time: 4 seconds 820 msec
Ended Job = job_201305061901_0002
MapReduce Jobs Launched:
Job 0: Map: 1Cumulative CPU: 4.82 sec HDFS Read: 53239663 HDFS
Write: 218 SUCCESS
Total MapReduce CPU Time Spent: 4 seconds 820 msec
OK
host identity user time size referer status agent
216.185.64.79 - - [18/Sep/2009:00:00:55 -0800] "GET /SELECT * FROM
users WHERE username = '' having 1=1-- HTTP/1.1" 200 3164 "-"
"Mozilla/5.0 (compatible; Feedfetcher-Google; (+http://www.google.
com/feedfetcher.html)"
Time taken: 11.572 seconds
hive>
```

We can see that there was one entry that had a commonly used method of SQL injection within the request field. The injection code appears simply as: ""GET / SELECT * FROM users WHERE username = " having 1=1--." Generally, the first element in the string would be a reference to a Web page, but the principle is the same. We simplified this example for clarity in explaining to you what was happening.

In this case, the main advantage of using Hive and other similar searches is that our search found the single known incident within all of these many server logs in very little time. Otherwise, it could be a seemingly endless search, with a "needle in a haystack" effort.

Directory Traversal and File Inclusion

Attackers may also attempt to add additional elements at the end of a URL query line to traverse the server's file system. Once the attackers locate the key folders and files, valuable information such as passwords may be retrieved, executable files could be added to the system, or the system could be vandalized.

We use the below-listed query searches within the request field for keywords related to directories at the root level of the file system.One part of the query also searches for the ubiquitous double dot characters (hidden folders), which are often used in these kinds of attacks. Although we mainly focus on terms and characters related to a Linux operating system, we also include some Windows-based terms and characters such as "c:\," ".exe," and ".ini."

```
SELECT * FROM apachelog
WHERE LOWER(request) LIKE '%usr/%'
OR LOWER(request) LIKE '%~/%'
OR LOWER(request) LIKE '%.exe%'
OR LOWER(request) LIKE '%.ini%'
OR LOWER(request) LIKE '%usr/%'
OR LOWER(request) LIKE '%etc/%'
--OR LOWER(request) LIKE '%home/%'
--OR LOWER(request) LIKE '%bin/%'
OR LOWER(request) LIKE '%dev/%'
OR LOWER(request) LIKE '%opt/%'
OR LOWER(request) LIKE '%root/%'
OR LOWER(request) LIKE '%sys/%'
OR LOWER(request) LIKE '%boot/%'
OR LOWER(request) LIKE '%mnt/%'
OR LOWER(request) LIKE '%proc/%'
OR LOWER(request) LIKE '%sbin/%'
OR LOWER(request) LIKE '%srv/%'
OR LOWER(request) LIKE '%var/%'
OR LOWER(request) LIKE '%c:\%'
OR LOWER(request) LIKE '%..%';
```

The results from running the query are shown below.

```
hive> SELECT * FROM apachelog
   > WHERE LOWER(request) LIKE '%usr/%'
   > OR LOWER(request) LIKE '%~/%'
   > OR LOWER(request) LIKE '%.exe%'
   > OR LOWER(request) LIKE '%.ini%'
   > OR LOWER(request) LIKE '%usr/%'
   > OR LOWER(request) LIKE '%etc/%'
   > --OR LOWER(request) LIKE '%home/%'
   > --OR LOWER(request) LIKE '%bin/%'
   > OR LOWER(request) LIKE '%dev/%'
   > OR LOWER(request) LIKE '%opt/%'
   > OR LOWER(request) LIKE '%root/%'
   > OR LOWER(request) LIKE '%sys/%'
   > OR LOWER(request) LIKE '%boot/%'
   > OR LOWER(request) LIKE '%mnt/%'
   > OR LOWER(request) LIKE '%proc/%'
   > OR LOWER(request) LIKE '%sbin/%'
   > OR LOWER(request) LIKE '%srv/%'
   > OR LOWER(request) LIKE '%var/%'
   > OR LOWER(request) LIKE '%c:\%'
   > OR LOWER(request) LIKE '%..%';
Total MapReduce jobs = 1
Launching Job 1 out of 1
```

```
Number of reduce tasks is set to 0 since there's no reduce operator
Starting Job = job_201305061901_0003, Tracking URL = http://local-
host.localdomain:50030/jobdetails.jsp?jobid=job_201305061901_0003>
Kill Command = /usr/lib/hadoop/bin/hadoop job -kill
job_201305061901_0003
Hadoop job information for Stage-1: number of mappers: 1; number of
reducers: 0
2013-05-06 20:32:02,894 Stage-1 map = 0%, reduce = 0%
2013-05-06 20:32:10,931 Stage-1 map = 83%, reduce = 0%
2013-05-06 20:32:11,937 Stage-1 map = 100%, reduce = 0%, Cumulative
CPU 7.58 sec
2013-05-06 20:32:12,944 Stage-1 map = 100%, reduce = 0%, Cumulative
CPU 7.58 sec
2013-05-06 20:32:13,956 Stage-1 map = 100%, reduce = 100%,
Cumulative CPU 7.58 sec
MapReduce Total cumulative CPU time: 7 seconds 580 msec
Ended Job = job_201305061901_0003
MapReduce Jobs Launched:
Job 0: Map: 1 Cumulative CPU: 7.58 sec HDFS Read: 53239663 HDFS
Write: 855 SUCCESS
Total MapReduce CPU Time Spent: 7 seconds 580 msec
OK
host identity user time size referer status agent
10.255.255.124 - - [25/Apr/2013:15:31:46 -0400] "GET /cgi-bin/
powerup/r.cgi?FILE=../../../../../../../../../../../etc/passwd
HTTP/1.1" 404 539 "-" "Mozilla/4.75 (Nikto/2.1.4) (Evasions:None)
(Test:003175)"
10.255.255.124 - - [25/Apr/2013:15:31:46 -0400] "GET /cgi-bin/r.
cgi?FILE=../../../../../../../../../../../etc/passwd HTTP/1.1" 404 531
"-" "Mozilla/4.75 (Nikto/2.1.4) (Evasions:None) (Test:003176)"
216.185.64.79 - - [18/Sep/2009:00:00:55 -0800] "GET /example.com/
doc/..%5c../Windows/System32/cmd.exe?/c+dir+c:\ HTTP/1.1" 200 3164
"-" "Mozilla/5.0 (compatible) Feedfetcher-Google; (+">http://www.
google.com/feedfetcher.html)"
216.185.64.79 - - [18/Sep/2009:00:00:55 -0800] "GET /example.com/
example.asp?display=../../../../../Windows/system.ini HTTP/1.1" 200
3164 "-" "Mozilla/5.0 (compatible) Feedfetcher-Google; (+">http://
www.google.com/feedfetcher.html)"
Time taken: 13.626 seconds
hive>
```

We found several examples of this attack attempt that were found with this query. Note that the status showed errors for a couple of the attempts, as seen by the status codes 404 and 531. However, you can see that two of the attempts succeeded, as evidenced by the status code 200. Notice also, the keywords "etc," "exe," "ini," and the use of the double dot navigation. Additionally, the file traversal to the "etc" directory appears to be related to an attempt to get at the "passwd" file—a commonly attempted attack vector.

Cross-site Request Forgery

The keywords found in this attack pertain to the browser's JavaScript alert notice.

```
SELECT * FROM apachelog
WHERE LOWER(request) LIKE '%>alert%'
OR LOWER(request) LIKE '%vulnerable%';

hive> SELECT * FROM apachelog
    > WHERE LOWER(request) LIKE '%>alert%'
    > OR LOWER(request) LIKE '%vulnerable%';
Total MapReduce jobs = 1
Launching Job 1 out of 1
Number of reduce tasks is set to 0 since there's no reduce
operator
Starting Job = job_201305071923_0007, Tracking URL = http://
localhost.localdomain:50030/jobdetails.jsp?jobid=job_
201305071923_0007
Kill Command = /usr/lib/hadoop/bin/hadoop job -kill
job_201305071923_0007
Hadoop job information for Stage-1: number of mappers: 1; number of
reducers: 0
2013-05-07 22:37:45,751 Stage-1 map = 0%, reduce = 0%
2013-05-07 22:37:53,784 Stage-1 map = 100%, reduce = 0%, Cumulative
CPU 7.01 sec
2013-05-07 22:37:54,796 Stage-1 map = 100%, reduce = 100%,
Cumulative CPU 7.01 sec
MapReduce Total cumulative CPU time: 7 seconds 10 msec
Ended Job = job_201305071923_0007
MapReduce Jobs Launched:
Job 0: Map: 1 Cumulative CPU: 7.01 sec HDFS Read: 159723693 HDFS
Write: 2428 SUCCESS
Total MapReduce CPU Time Spent: 7 seconds 10 msec
OK
host identity user time request status size referer agent
10.255.255.124 - - [25/Apr/2013:15:31:46 -0400] "GET /options.
php?optpage=<script>alert('Vulnerable!')</script> HTTP/1.1"
404 529 "-" "Mozilla/4.75 (Nikto/2.1.4) (Evasions:None)
(Test:003171)"
10.255.255.124 - - [25/Apr/2013:15:31:46 -0400] "GET /search.php?ma
ilbox=INBOX&what=x&where=<script>alert('Vulnerable!')</script>&
submit=Search HTTP/1.1" 404 528 "-" "Mozilla/4.75 (Nikto/2.1.4)
(Evasions:None) (Test:003172)"
10.255.255.124 - - [25/Apr/2013:15:31:46 -0400] "GET /help.
php?chapter=<script>alert('Vulnerable')</script> HTTP/1.1"
404 526 "-" "Mozilla/4.75 (Nikto/2.1.4) (Evasions:None)
(Test:003173)"
```

You can see there are several log entries having triggered the JavaScript alert notice.

Command Injection

This attack tries to disguise commands with HTML URL encoding. The following query includes keywords for some common examples.

```
SELECT * FROM apachelog
WHERE LOWER(request) LIKE '%&comma%'
OR LOWER(request) LIKE '%20echo%'
OR LOWER(request) LIKE '%60id%';

hive> SELECT * FROM apachelog
   > WHERE LOWER(request) LIKE '%&comma%'
   > OR LOWER(request) LIKE '%20echo%'
   > OR LOWER(request) LIKE '%60id%';
Total MapReduce jobs = 1
Launching Job 1 out of 1
Number of reduce tasks is set to 0 since there's no reduce operator
Starting Job = job_201305071923_0005, Tracking URL = http://local-
host.localdomain:50030/jobdetails.jsp?jobid=job_201305071923_0005>
Kill Command = /usr/lib/hadoop/bin/hadoop job -kill
job_201305071923_0005
Hadoop job information for Stage-1: number of mappers: 1; number of
reducers: 0
2013-05-07 22:28:42,343 Stage-1 map = 0%, reduce = 0%
2013-05-07 22:28:51,378 Stage-1 map = 83%, reduce = 0%
2013-05-07 22:28:52,384 Stage-1 map = 100%, reduce = 0%, Cumulative
CPU 8.09 sec
2013-05-07 22:28:53,394 Stage-1 map = 100%, reduce = 100%,
Cumulative CPU 8.09 sec
MapReduce Total cumulative CPU time: 8 seconds 90 msec
Ended Job = job_201305071923_0005
MapReduce Jobs Launched:
Job 0: Map: 1 Cumulative CPU: 8.09 sec HDFS Read: 159723693 HDFS
Write: 6080 SUCCESS
Total MapReduce CPU Time Spent: 8 seconds 90 msec
OK
host identity user time request status size referer agent
10.255.255.124 - - [25/Apr/2013:15:31:46 -0400] "GET /forums-
calendar.php?calbirthdays=1&action=getday&day=2001-8-15&com-
ma=%22;echo%20'';%20echo%20%60id%20%60;die();echo%22 HTTP/1.1" 404
536 "-" "Mozilla/4.75 (Nikto/2.1.4) (Evasions:None) (Test:003039)"
10.255.255.124 - - [25/Apr/2013:15:31:46 -0400] "GET /forumz-
calendar.php?calbirthdays=1&action=getday&day=2001-8-15&com-
ma=%22;echo%20'';%20echo%20%60id%20%60;die();echo%22 HTTP/1.1" 404
536 "-" "Mozilla/4.75 (Nikto/2.1.4) (Evasions:None) (Test:003040)"
10.255.255.124 - - [25/Apr/2013:15:31:46 -0400] "GET /htforum-
calendar.php?calbirthdays=1&action=getday&day=2001-8-15&com-
ma=%22;echo%20'';%20echo%20%60id%20%60;die();echo%22 HTTP/1.1" 404
537 "-" "Mozilla/4.75 (Nikto/2.1.4) (Evasions:None) (Test:003041)"
10.255.255.124 - - [25/Apr/2013:15:31:46 -0400] "GET /vbcalendar.
php?calbirthdays=1&action=getday&day=2001-8-15&comma=%22;echo%20
```

```
''%;20echo%20%60id%20%60;die();echo%22 HTTP/1.1" 404 532 "-"
"Mozilla/4.75 (Nikto/2.1.4) (Evasions:None) (Test:003042)"
10.255.255.124 - - [25/Apr/2013:15:31:46 -0400] "GET /vbullet-
incalendar.php?calbirthdays=1&action=getday&day=2001-8-15&com-
ma=%22;echo%20''%;20echo%20%60id%20%60;die();echo%22 HTTP/1.1" 404
539 "-" "Mozilla/4.75 (Nikto/2.1.4) (Evasions:None) (Test:003043)"
10.255.255.124 - - [25/Apr/2013:15:31:46 -0400] "GET /cgi-bin/
calendar.php?calbirthdays=1&action=getday&day=2001-8-15&com-
ma=%22;echo%20''%;20echo%20%60id%20%60;die();echo%22 HTTP/1.1" 404
538 "-" "Mozilla/4.75 (Nikto/2.1.4) (Evasions:None) (Test:003044)"
Time taken: 13.51 seconds
```

MySQL Charset Switch and MS-SQL DoS Attack

This attack involves altering the character set to evade the built-in validation functionality of databases and can be used in a denial of service attack (DoS). Keywords in this attack that are related to changing the character set of a table or column include "alter," "character," and "set." Other keywords that are commonly found in DoS attacks include "waitfor," "time," and "goto."

```
SELECT * FROM apachelog
WHERE LOWER(request) LIKE '%alter%'
AND LOWER(request) LIKE '%character%'
AND LOWER(request) LIKE '%set%';

SELECT * FROM apachelog
WHERE LOWER(request) LIKE '%waitfor%'
AND LOWER(request) LIKE '%time%';

SELECT * FROM apachelog
WHERE LOWER(request) LIKE '%goto%';
```

All three queries were run together at the same time from the Hive command line. The results are shown below. You will see a single log entry, where the attacker changed the character set to gbk_chinese_ci. We did not find any examples from which to test the other two queries, but they should function similarly.

```
hive> SELECT * FROM apachelog
   > WHERE LOWER(request) LIKE '%alter%'
   > AND LOWER(request) LIKE '%character%'
   > AND LOWER(request) LIKE '%set%';
Total MapReduce jobs = 1
Launching Job 1 out of 1
Number of reduce tasks is set to 0 since there's no reduce operator
Starting Job = job_201305061901_0005, Tracking URL = http://local-
host.localdomain:50030/jobdetails.jsp?jobid=job_201305061901_0005
Kill Command = /usr/lib/hadoop/bin/hadoop job -kill
job_201305061901_0005
Hadoop job information for Stage-1: number of mappers: 1; number of
reducers: 0
```

```
2013-05-06 21:07:52,856 Stage-1 map = 0%, reduce = 0%
2013-05-06 21:07:57,880 Stage-1 map = 100%, reduce = 0%, Cumulative
CPU 2.82 sec
2013-05-06 21:07:58,886 Stage-1 map = 100%, reduce = 0%, Cumulative
CPU 2.82 sec
2013-05-06 21:07:59,897 Stage-1 map = 100%, reduce = 100%,
Cumulative CPU 2.82 sec
MapReduce Total cumulative CPU time: 2 seconds 820 msec
Ended Job = job_201305061901_0005
MapReduce Jobs Launched:
Job 0: Map: 1 Cumulative CPU: 2.82 sec HDFS Read: 53239663 HDFS
Write: 277 SUCCESS
Total MapReduce CPU Time Spent: 2 seconds 820 msec OK
216.185.64.79 - - [18/Sep/2009:00:00:55 -0800] "GET /ALTER TABLE
'users' CHANGE 'password' 'password' VARCHAR(255) CHARACTER SET gbk
COLLATE gbk_chinese_ci NOT NULL HTTP/1.1" 200 3164 "-" "Mozilla/5.0
(compatible) Feedfetcher-Google; (+http://www.google.com/
feedfetcher.html)"
Time taken: 9.927 seconds
hive>
    > SELECT * FROM apachelog
    > WHERE LOWER(request) LIKE '%waitfor%'
    > AND LOWER(request) LIKE '%time%';
Total MapReduce jobs = 1
Launching Job 1 out of 1
Number of reduce tasks is set to 0 since there's no reduce operator
Starting Job = job_201305061901_0006, Tracking URL = http://local-
host.localdomain:50030/jobdetails.jsp?jobid=job_201305061901_0006
Kill Command = /usr/lib/hadoop/bin/hadoop job -kill
job_201305061901_0006
Hadoop job information for Stage-1: number of mappers: 1; number of
reducers: 0
2013-05-06 21:08:02,294 Stage-1 map = 0%, reduce = 0%
2013-05-06 21:08:08,318 Stage-1 map = 100%, reduce = 0%, Cumulative
CPU 2.75 sec
2013-05-06 21:08:09,328 Stage-1 map = 100%, reduce = 100%,
Cumulative CPU 2.75 sec
MapReduce Total cumulative CPU time: 2 seconds 750 msec
Ended Job = job_201305061901_0006
MapReduce Jobs Launched:
Job 0: Map: 1 Cumulative CPU: 2.75 sec HDFS Read: 53239663 HDFS
Write: 0 SUCCESS
Total MapReduce CPU Time Spent: 2 seconds 750 msec
OK
Time taken: 9.437 seconds
hive>
  > SELECT * FROM apachelog
  > WHERE LOWER(request) LIKE '%goto%';
Total MapReduce jobs = 1
```

```
Launching Job 1 out of 1
Number of reduce tasks is set to 0 since there's no reduce operator
Starting Job = job_201305061901_0007, Tracking URL = http://local-
host.localdomain:50030/jobdetails.jsp?jobid=job_201305061901_0007
Kill Command = /usr/lib/hadoop/bin/hadoop job -kill
job_201305061901_0007
Hadoop job information for Stage-1: number of mappers: 1; number of
reducers: 0
2013-05-06 21:08:23,417 Stage-1 map = 0%, reduce = 0%
2013-05-06 21:08:28,438 Stage-1 map = 100%, reduce = 0%, Cumulative
CPU 2.72 sec
2013-05-06 21:08:29,450 Stage-1 map = 100%, reduce = 100%,
Cumulative CPU 2.72 sec
MapReduce Total cumulative CPU time: 2 seconds 720 msec
Ended Job = job_201305061901_0007
MapReduce Jobs Launched:
Job 0: Map: 1 Cumulative CPU: 2.72 sec HDFS Read: 53239663 HDFS
Write: 0 SUCCESS
Total MapReduce CPU Time Spent: 2 seconds 720 msec
OK
Time taken: 8.413 seconds
```

Tallying and Tracking Failed Request Statuses

As was seen in one of the query results above, attack attempts can result in status codes indicating both success and failure. However, often an attacker may experience a number of failures before hitting upon the right combination that results in a success.

We can sort hosts sending requests to determine which IP addresses produce the most failures. While a high number of failures are not a definitive indication that an attack has taken place, it could serve as a starting point for further investigation. Aside from security concerns, it could also help to identify where users are having difficulty with the system, as well as those IP addresses that may be putting the system under the greatest stress.

Hosts with the most Failed Requests

The status indicators in server logs are shown as three-digit codes. Codes in the 100, 200, or 300 series range indicate successful client requests and server responses. However, while codes in the 400 range indicate failed requests, the 500 range indicates failed responses due to problems on the server side. A series of failed requests could be an indication of an attacker using trial-and-error tactics until an attack succeeds. Failed server responses could be an indication that an attack has succeeded in doing server-side damage.

The following query groups failed requests by host, using Hive's case statements and the substring function, SUBSTR(). The function is written as "substr(status,1,1)." The function queries the status field for the first character, and also ends with the first character. In other words, the first digit indicates at which character the query should begin, and the second digit indicates how many characters to include, from left to right. Cases where the first digit in the status code is either a "4" or a "5" are coded as a "1" in a newly added "failed-access" column, while all other status codes are coded as a "0." As you will see, the resulting new view enables easy tallying of all failed requests as 1's and all successful requests as 0's.

You will see how a view is created in Hive in the same manner as a table. However, unlike a table, the view does not store any data within the Hadoop File System (HDFS), but only stores the query code. A view is used in this case as a step among a series of queries to generate the final results. One query builds upon the others. Also, you will see that Hive has a command to set the output to CSV when storing the results externally: set hive.io.output.fileformat = CSVTextFile. This command is used in the second query.

```
CREATE VIEW IF NOT EXISTS statusgroupings AS
SELECT host, identity, user, time, request, status, size, referer,
agent, CASE substr(status,1,1)
WHEN '1' THEN '0'
WHEN '2' THEN '0'
WHEN '3' THEN '0'
WHEN '4' THEN '1'
WHEN '5' THEN '1'
ELSE '0'
END
AS failedaccess
FROM apachelog;

--store the results of the preceding view
set hive.io.output.fileformat = CSVTextFile;
INSERT OVERWRITE LOCAL DIRECTORY '/mnt/hgfs/BigDataAnalytics/Proj-
ect1/ApacheLog' SELECT * FROM statusgroupings;

--sum total failed access attempts by host
CREATE VIEW IF NOT EXISTS FailedHostAttempts AS
SELECT host, SUM(failedaccess) AS failedAttempts
FROM statusgroupings
GROUP BY host
ORDER BY failedAttempts DESC;

--count total host attempts to access
CREATE VIEW IF NOT EXISTS TotalHostAttempts AS
SELECT host, count(host) AS hostAccessAttempts
FROM statusgroupings
GROUP BY host
ORDER BY hostAccessAttempts DESC;
```

From these views we can calculate the percentage of failed requests by host, as shown in the query below.

```
--top 20 proportions of failed attempts
SELECT a.host, failedAttempts, hostAccessAttempts, failedAttempts /
hostAccessAttempts AS percentFailed
FROM TotalHostAttempts a
JOIN FailedHostAttempts b
ON a.host = b.host
WHERE failedAttempts / hostAccessAttempts > 0
ORDER BY percentFailed DESC
LIMIT 20;
```

Since the chain of views above produces a large amount of command line, diagnostic related output from MapReduce, only the actual view results that are generated from the above query are shown below. As one might imagine, the highest percentages of failed requests tend to occur with hosts having made only a few requests or even one request. In most cases, these entries are not likely to be an issue. However, if we were to see a very large number of these requests, it might be an indication of a distributed DoS attack, where a bot is programmed to send access requests from many different IP addresses. As you can see, no such pattern is evident here in Amazon's data, and no such patterns were loaded into the sample attack log, access_log_7.

However, the second listed host, IP 10.255.255.124, does appear a bit suspicious with 12 access attempts and all 12 failing. This could warrant further investigation with an ad hoc query to drill into the requests made by this host.

```
Total MapReduce CPU Time Spent: 17 seconds 260 msec
OK
host failedattempts hostaccessattempts percentfailed
189.106.160.140    1.0   1      1.0
10.255.255.124    12.0   12     1.0
79.11.25.143       1.0   1      1.0
99.157.209.86      1.0   1      1.0
24.21.134.171      3.0   4      0.75
81.193.181.206     2.0   3      0.6666666666666666
87.238.130.200     4.0   7      0.5714285714285714
165.166.103.33     1.0   2      0.5
124.177.134.93     2.0   4      0.5
88.38.60.152       2.0   4      0.5
84.203.44.110      2.0   4      0.5
115.74.146.80      1.0   2      0.5
71.49.39.235       1.0   2      0.5
68.96.161.201      1.0   2      0.5
62.150.156.229     1.0   2      0.5
58.69.168.155      1.0   2      0.5
58.68.8.190        2.0   4      0.5
41.100.138.220     1.0   2      0.5
```

```
4.131.17.243        1.0   2    0.5
201.43.250.154      1.0   2    0.5
Time taken: 64.786 seconds
```

The following query modifies the query above so that only the hosts having at least 20 log entries are shown. The top listed IP, 221.221.9.60, has had 28% of its requests fail. This could also warrant further investigation. If upon further querying we were to find many failed access attempts, followed by a string of successes, this could be an indication of an attack.

```
--top 20 proportions of failed attempts where more than 20 attempts
total
SELECT a.host, failedAttempts, hostAccessAttempts, failedAttempts /
hostAccessAttempts AS percentFailed
FROM TotalHostAttempts a
JOIN FailedHostAttempts b
ON a.host = b.host
WHERE failedAttempts / hostAccessAttempts > 0
AND hostAccessAttempts > 20
ORDER BY percentFailed DESC
LIMIT 20;

Total MapReduce CPU Time Spent: 16 seconds 880 msec
OK
host failedattempts hostaccessattempts percentfailed
221.221.9.60    14.0    50    0.28
41.202.75.35     5.0    26    0.19230769230769232
41.178.112.197  17.0    89    0.19101123595505617
121.205.226.76  63.0   334    0.18862275449101795
114.200.199.144  5.0    27    0.18518518518518517
78.178.233.22    5.0    27    0.18518518518518517
216.24.131.152  12.0    66    0.18181818181818182
68.42.128.66     4.0    22    0.18181818181818182
201.2.78.10      4.0    24    0.16666666666666666
194.141.2.1      4.0    24    0.16666666666666666
194.110.194.1    5.0    30    0.16666666666666666
69.122.96.121    4.0    24    0.16666666666666666
68.117.200.60    4.0    24    0.16666666666666666
76.122.81.132    4.0    25    0.16
79.66.21.60      6.0    38    0.15789473684210525
24.183.197.231   3.0    21    0.14285714285714285
68.193.125.219   4.0    28    0.14285714285714285
149.6.164.150    6.0    43    0.13953488372093023
99.141.88.139    3.0    22    0.13636363636363635
15.203.233.77    3.0    22    0.13636363636363635
Time taken: 65.271 seconds
```

For those who may be curious, we also ran a query on IP 221.221.9.60, ordering it by month and day. Time aggregations will be discussed later in this chapter.

However, all of the failed requests came from a "404 file not found" error, which occurred repeatedly, while trying to access "favicon.ico." Modern browsers will automatically send requests to seek an icon that would appear to the left of the URL, which is known as a favicon. If the browser cannot find a favicon, an error message could be generated and is likely the cause of these "404 file not found" errors. The drill-down query was in the form, "select * from by_month where host in('221.221.9.60') order by monthday;". The by_month view and the monthday field will be discussed in more detail later in the chapter.

Bot Activity

A great deal of bot activity can be found within server logs, most of it legitimate. Bots such as those from search engines crawl the Internet to build indexes, such as those deployed by Google and Microsoft. The bots advertise themselves as bots in the agent log field. While an illegitimate bot may be a bit more clandestine, masquerading as a legitimate bot could also be an effective attack strategy.

The next query we will introduce searches for the key term "bot" in the agent field. It returns a list of bot agents, along with a count of the number of log entries for each agent. Even if the bots are legitimate, it is interesting to see the volume of bot activity on these servers. Some of the agents are easily recognizable, while others may not be as recognizable. As such, some may warrant further research as to their origins.

```
--bot activity
SELECT agent, count(agent) AS hits
FROM apachelog
WHERE agent LIKE '%bot%'
GROUP BY agent
ORDER BY hits DESC;
Total MapReduce CPU Time Spent: 6 seconds 920 msec
OK
agent hits
"Mozilla/5.0 (compatible; Googlebot/2.1; +http://www.google.com/
bot.html)" 45528
"msnbot/2.0b (+http://search.msn.com/msnbot.htm)" 9248
"msnbot/1.1 (+http://search.msn.com/msnbot.htm)" 8400.
"Mozilla/5.0 (Twiceler-0.9 http://www.cuil.com/twiceler/robot.
html)" 4571
"Googlebot-Image/1.0" 4543
"Mozilla/5.0 (X11; U; Linux i686; en-US; rv:1.2.1; aggre-
gator:Spinn3r (Spinn3r 3.1); http://spinn3r.com/robot)
Gecko/20021130" 2431
"Mozilla/5.0 (Windows; U; Windows NT 5.1; fr; rv:1.8.1) VoilaBot
BETA 1.2 (support.voilabot@orange-ftgroup.com)" 382
"OOZBOT/0.20 ( http://www.setooz.com/oozbot.html ; agentname at
setooz dot_com )" 169
```

```
"Mozilla/5.0 (compatible; Tagoobot/3.0; +http://www.tagoo.ru)" 102
"Mozilla/5.0 (compatible; discobot/1.1; +http://discoveryengine.
com/discobot.html)" 56
"Mozilla/4.0 (compatible; MSIE 6.0; Windows NT 5.1; SV1;
http://www.changedetection.com/bot.html )" 49
"SAMSUNG-SGH-E250/1.0 Profile/MIDP-2.0 Configuration/CLDC-1.1
UP.Browser/6.2.3.3.c.1.101 (GUI) MMP/2.0 (compatible; Googlebot-
Mobile/2.1; +http://www.google.com/bot.html)" 32
"Mozilla/5.0 (compatible; Exabot/3.0; +http://www.exabot.com/go/
robot)" 29
"Gaisbot/3.0+(robot06@gais.cs.ccu.edu.tw;+http://gais.cs.ccu.edu.
tw/robot.php)" 27
"FollowSite Bot (  http://www.followsite.com/bot.html  )" 18
"Gigabot/3.0 (http://www.gigablast.com/spider.html)" 13
"MLBot (www.metadatalabs.com/mlbot)" 10
"Mozilla/5.0 (compatible; MJ12bot/v1.2.5; http://www.majestic12.
co.uk/bot.php?+)" 10
"Yeti/1.0 (NHN Corp.; http://help.naver.com/robots/)" 9
"psbot/0.1 (+http://www.picsearch.com/bot.html)" 8
"Mozilla/5.0 (compatible; seexie.com_bot/4.1; +http://www.seexie.
com)" 6
"Mozilla/5.0 (compatible; Exabot-Images/3.0; +http://www.exabot.
com/go/robot)" 5
"Mozilla/5.0 (compatible; BuzzRankingBot/1.0; +http://www.
buzzrankingbot.
com/)" 4
"DoCoMo/2.0 N905i(c100;TB;W24H16) (compatible; Googlebot-
Mobile/2.1; +http://www.google.com/bot.html)" 4
Time taken: 23.632 seconds
```

We can modify this query to only show instances where bot agent requests resulted in either a failed client request or a failed server response. In this case, the agents having the most failed requests are prominent, well-known bots having high volumes, such as Google or MSN. Some of these requests apparently occurred at a time when there was an internal server error, as given by the status code "505." You will see, though, that this query only extracts the maximum code as a sample. The query could be easily modified to search for specified error types, such as "404," which indicates that the file was not found. We did not have known bot threats loaded into the sample logs. However, bot activity may be worth investigating, as there have been known cases where, for example, attackers have tried to exploit a Wordpress plugin by uploading a shell. While trying to find where the shell is located, the attacker could generate numerous "404 file not found" errors. This query could be useful in beginning a search for such potential threats, should they occur. Also, it could be useful to monitor the volume of bot activity and any related issues they may cause for the server, even if the activity is not intended to be malicious.

```
SELECT agent, count(agent) AS hits, MAX(status) AS sampleStatus
FROM apachelog
WHERE agent LIKE '%bot%'
AND substr(status,1,1) IN ('4','5')
GROUP BY agent
ORDER BY hits DESC
LIMIT 20;

Total MapReduce CPU Time Spent: 7 seconds 190 msec
OK
agent hitssamplestatus
"Mozilla/5.0 (compatible; Googlebot/2.1; +http://www.google.com/
bot.html)"272500
"Mozilla/5.0 (Twiceler-0.9 http://www.cuil.com/twiceler/robot.
html)"225500
"msnbot/2.0b (+http://search.msn.com/msnbot.htm)"88500
"msnbot/1.1 (+http://search.msn.com/msnbot.htm)"82500
"Googlebot-Image/1.0"74500
Time taken: 31.764 seconds
```

Time Aggregations

The queries in this section parse the time field in the server log, so as to be able to evaluate server activity over time. The time field appears in the log file as "[20/Jul/2009:20:12:22 -0700]." In this case, the first digit, "20," is the day, which is followed by the month, "Jul," and the year, "2009." Three sets of numbers follow the year, which are separated by a colon. These represent the hour, minute, and second, respectively. The final four digits following the dash represent the time zone.

We use the query below, SUBSTR() function, to parse the day, month, and year. We then convert the month to a two-digit format and reassemble the order, so the year precedes month and month precedes day. This reassembly is accomplished with the CONCAT() function, which concatenates strings together into the desired order. This new ordering allows for easier sorting of the date. As you will see, the result of the query allows for subsequent queries to easily aggregate results by year, month, day, or any combination of these.

```
CREATE VIEW IF NOT EXISTS by_month AS
SELECT host, identity, user, time, CASE substr(time,5,3)
WHEN 'Jan' THEN '01'
WHEN 'Feb' THEN '02'
WHEN 'Mar' THEN '03'
WHEN 'Apr' THEN '04'
WHEN 'May' THEN '05'
WHEN 'Jun' THEN '06'
WHEN 'Jul' THEN '07'
WHEN 'Aug' THEN '08'
```

```
WHEN 'Sep' THEN '09'
WHEN 'Oct' THEN '10'
WHEN 'Nov' THEN '11'
WHEN 'Dec' THEN '12'
ELSE '00'
END
AS month, substr(time,9,4) AS year, concat(substr(time,9,4), CASE
substr(time,5,3)
WHEN 'Jan' THEN '01'
WHEN 'Feb' THEN '02'
WHEN 'Mar' THEN '03'
WHEN 'Apr' THEN '04'
WHEN 'May' THEN '05'
WHEN 'Jun' THEN '06'
WHEN 'Jul' THEN '07'
WHEN 'Aug' THEN '08'
WHEN 'Sep' THEN '09'
WHEN 'Oct' THEN '10'
WHEN 'Nov' THEN '11'
WHEN 'Dec' THEN '12'
ELSE '00'
END) AS yearmonth, concat(CASE substr(time,5,3)
WHEN 'Jan' THEN '01'
WHEN 'Feb' THEN '02'
WHEN 'Mar' THEN '03'
WHEN 'Apr' THEN '04'
WHEN 'May' THEN '05'
WHEN 'Jun' THEN '06'
WHEN 'Jul' THEN '07'
WHEN 'Aug' THEN '08'
WHEN 'Sep' THEN '09'
WHEN 'Oct' THEN '10'
WHEN 'Nov' THEN '11'
WHEN 'Dec' THEN '12'
ELSE '00'
END,substr(time,2,2)) AS monthday, request, status, size, referer,
agent
FROM apachelog;
```

We used the "by_month" query view to parse the time column to produce several new columns, as shown by running the select query below. There is now a column for month, year, monthday, and yearmonth.

```
hive> SELECT time, month, year, monthday, yearmonth FROM by_month
LIMIT 1;
Total MapReduce jobs = 1
Launching Job 1 out of 1
Number of reduce tasks is set to 0 since there's no reduce operator
Starting Job = job_201305061901_0045, Tracking URL = http://local-
host.localdomain:50030/jobdetails.jsp?jobid=job_201305061901_0045>
```

```
Kill Command = /usr/lib/hadoop/bin/hadoop job -kill
job_201305061901_0045
Hadoop job information for Stage-1: number of mappers: 1; number of
reducers: 0
2013-05-07 13:17:27,444 Stage-1 map = 0%, reduce = 0%
2013-05-07 13:17:31,458 Stage-1 map = 100%, reduce = 0%, Cumulative
CPU 1.36 sec
2013-05-07 13:17:32,464 Stage-1 map = 100%, reduce = 0%, Cumulative
CPU 1.36 sec
2013-05-07 13:17:33,471 Stage-1 map = 100%, reduce = 100%, Cumula-
tive CPU 1.36 sec
MapReduce Total cumulative CPU time: 1 seconds 360 msec
Ended Job = job_201305061901_0045
MapReduce Jobs Launched:
Job 0: Map: 1 Cumulative CPU: 1.36 sec HDFS Read: 66093 HDFS Write:
490 SUCCESS
Total MapReduce CPU Time Spent: 1 seconds 360 msec
OK
time month year monthday yearmonth
[20/Jul/2009:20:12:22 -0700] 07 2009 0720 200907
Time taken: 9.398 seconds
```

We can now use this view to produce a variety of time aggregations. We would
like to share a few ideas to serve as possible starting points for follow-up queries. As with any of the queries suggested in this chapter, the results can be
written to a local directory for further analysis, if desired. To do so, you simply
precede the selected statement with the below-listed query. Of course, the local
directory specified should be changed to match the directory on your system
where the results will be stored.

```
INSERT OVERWRITE LOCAL DIRECTORY '/mnt/hgfs/BigDataAnalytics/
Project1/TopHostFailedLogongsByDay'
```

For the purpose of our demonstration, these queries simply write results to the
screen, and the result sets are limited to only 10 rows.

Hosts with the most Failed Requests per day, or per month

Next we will use a query to show the number of failed query attempts, grouped
by day and host. The below-listed query shows the hosts that had the highest
numbers of failed requests in a day, along with the day and month in which they
occurred. If there were a very high number of requests for a given host IP on any
given day, it could be an indication of an attack attempt, such as a DoS attack.
In this case, since the log samples were not loaded with any known DoS attack
examples, we see that the IP hosts with the highest counts of failed requests per
day are also the same hosts that tend to produce a great many requests overall.

```
--Show hosts sorted by frequency of failed calls to server by day
SELECT monthday, host, COUNT(host) AS host_freq
FROM by_month
```

```
WHERE substr(status,1,1) IN('4','5')
GROUP BY monthday, host
ORDER BY host_freq DESC
LIMIT 10;
```

You can see the result of this query, which is shown below. (Spacing was added to the columns to make them easier to read.)

```
monthday  host            host_freq
0724      121.205.226.76  57
0807      66.249.67.3     31
0727      66.249.67.3     27
0723      38.99.44.101    27
0724      72.30.142.87    25
0910      66.249.67.3     24
0724      66.249.67.3     24
0927      66.249.67.3     22
0926      66.249.67.3     20
0723      .30.142.87      20
Time taken: 21.697 seconds
```

Below is a similar query, except that it aggregates results by month, rather than day.

```
--Show hosts sorted by frequency of failed calls to server by month
SELECT yearmonth, host, COUNT(host) AS host_freq
FROM by_month
WHERE substr(status,1,1) IN('4','5')
GROUP BY yearmonth, host
ORDER BY host_freq DESC
LIMIT 10;

yearmonth  host            host_freq
200908     66.249.67.3     437
200909     66.249.67.3     433
200909     74.125.74.193   184
200908     64.233.172.17   180
200907     66.249.67.3     178
200909     74.125.16.65    172
200908     72.14.192.65    171
200908     74.125.74.193   169
200908     66.249.67.87    169
200908     74.125.16.65    169
Time taken: 21.694 seconds
```

Failed Requests Presented as a Monthly Time Series

Next we will examine a query view aggregating the number of failed requests, regardless of the host source, as a time series by month and year. This query is stored as a view for our later use, to calculate a ratio of failed to successful requests.

```
--Unsuccessful server calls as a time series by year and month
Create VIEW FailedRequestsTimeSeriesByMonth AS
SELECT yearmonth, COUNT(yearmonth) AS failedrequest_freq
FROM by_month
WHERE substr(status,1,1) IN('4','5')
GROUP BY yearmonth
ORDER BY yearmonth ASC;
SELECT * FROM FailedRequestsTimeSeriesByMonth;
```

We show the result as shown. As you can see, there is a spike in the number of failed requests in August and September of 2009.

```
yearmonth failedrequest_freq
200907    1861
200908    2848
200909    2706
200910    55
Time taken: 23.682 seconds
```

It is possible that the increase in failed requests in August and September was due to an increase in Web traffic, in general. To determine this, we can run the same query without the filter or we can also filter on just the successful requests. We use the below-listed query to tally the successful requests by month.

```
--Successful server calls as a time series by year and month
Create VIEW SuccessfulRequestsTimeSeriesByMonth AS
SELECT yearmonth, COUNT(yearmonth) AS successfulrequest_freq
FROM by_month
WHERE substr(status,1,1) IN('1','2','3')
GROUP BY yearmonth
ORDER BY yearmonth ASC;
SELECT * FROM SuccessfulRequestsTimeSeriesByMonth;
```

Based on the results below, we can see that, indeed, the volume of successful requests went up substantially in August and September. So, it is likely that the number of failed requests for those months may have been in-line with the overall request volume. We will check our assumption next.

```
yearmonth    failedrequest_freq
200907       57972
200908       88821
200909       83185
200910       1902
Time taken: 21.619 seconds
```

Ratio of Failed to Successful Requests as a Time Series

To see if the volume of failed requests is, indeed, proportional to what would be expected, given the number of successful requests, we use the query below to calculate a ratio of failed requests to successful requests. We combine the two views above using a JOIN statement.

```
SELECT a.yearmonth, failedrequest_freq / successfulrequest_freq AS
failratio
FROM FailedRequestsTimeSeries a
JOIN SuccessfulRequestsTimeSeries b
ON a.yearmonth = b.yearmonth
ORDER BY yearmonth ASC;

yearmonth  failratio
200907     0.03210170427102739
200908     0.03206448925366749
200909     0.032529903227745384
200910     0.028916929547844375
Time taken: 66.867 seconds
```

We note that the ratio has held rather constant from month to month at around 0.03. This suggests that the number of failed requests each month is about what we would expect, given the volume of successful requests.

Of course, we could also run a query by day, as well, and this could reveal activity that could be obscured in a monthly aggregation. We use the query below, which combines the year, month, and day into a single string that can be sorted, in the form "20090720," where the first four digits represents the year, the next two are the month, and the last two digits are the day.

```
--enable the creation of a time series by day over multiple years
and months
CREATE VIEW by_day AS
SELECT host, identity, user, time, concat(year, monthday) AS
yearmonthday, request, status, size, referer, agent
FROM by_month;

SELECT * FROM by_day LIMIT 10;
```

The results of our query are shown below, giving the top 10 rows produced by the view. We can see that we now have a "yearmonthday" field in the desired format to enable aggregating and sorting by day, across multiple years and months.

```
host identity user time yearmonthday request status size referer agent
66.249.67.3 - - [20/Jul/2009:20:12:22 -0700] 20090720 "GET /
gallery/main.php?g2_controller=exif.SwitchDetailMode&g2_mode=-
detailed&g2_return=%2Fgallery%2Fmain.php%3Fg2_itemId%3D15741&g2_
returnName=photo HTTP/1.1"302 5 "-" "Mozilla/5.0 (compatible;
Googlebot/2.1; +>http://www.google.com/bot.html)
66.249.67.3 - - [20/Jul/2009:20:12:25 -0700] 20090720 "GET /gallery/
main.php?g2_itemId=15741&g2_fromNavId=x8fa12efc HTTP/1.1" 200 8068
"-" "Mozilla/5.0 (compatible; Googlebot/2.1; +>http://www.google.
com/bot.html)
```

```
64.233.172.17 - - [20/Jul/2009:20:12:26 -0700] 20090720 "GET /gwid-
gets/alexa.xml HTTP/1.1" 200 2969 "-" "Mozilla/5.0 (compatible)
Feedfetcher-Google; (+>http://www.google.com/feedfetcher.html)
74.125.74.193 - - [20/Jul/2009:20:13:01 -0700] 20090720 "GET /gwid-
gets/alexa.xml HTTP/1.1" 200 2969 "-" "Mozilla/5.0 (compatible)
Feedfetcher-Google; (+>http://www.google.com/feedfetcher.html)
192.168.1.198 - - [20/Jul/2009:20:13:18 -0700] 20090720 "GET /
HTTP/1.1" 200 17935 "-" "Mozilla/5.0 (Macintosh; U; Intel Mac OS X
10_5_7; en-us) AppleWebKit/530.17 (KHTML, like Gecko) Version/4.0
Safari/530.17"
192.168.1.198 - - [20/Jul/2009:20:13:18 -0700] 20090720 "GET /
style.css HTTP/1.1" 200 1504 "http://example.org/" "Mozilla/5.0
(Macintosh; U; Intel Mac OS X 10_5_7; en-us) AppleWebKit/530.17
(KHTML, like Gecko) Version/4.0 Safari/530.17"
192.168.1.198 - - [20/Jul/2009:20:13:19 -0700] 20090720 "GET
/favicon.ico HTTP/1.1" 404 146 "http://example.org/" "Mozilla/5.0
(Macintosh; U; Intel Mac OS X 10_5_7; en-us) AppleWebKit/530.17
(KHTML, like Gecko) Version/4.0 Safari/530.17"
66.249.67.3 - - [20/Jul/2009:20:13:21 -0700] 20090720 "GET /
gallery/main.php?g2_controller=exif.SwitchDetailMode&g2_mode=-
detailed&g2_return=%2Fgallery%2Fmain.php%3Fg2_itemId%3D30893&g2_
returnName=photo HTTP/1.1"302 5 "-" "Mozilla/5.0 (compatible;
Googlebot/2.1; +>http://www.google.com/bot.html)
66.249.67.3 - - [20/Jul/2009:20:13:24 -0700] 20090720 "GET /gallery/
main.php?g2_itemId=30893&g2_fromNavId=xfc647d65 HTTP/1.1" 200 8196
"-" "Mozilla/5.0 (compatible; Googlebot/2.1; +>http://www.google.
com/bot.html)
66.249.67.3 - - [20/Jul/2009:20:13:29 -0700] 20090720 "GET /
gallery/main.php?g2_view=search.SearchScan&g2_form%5BuseDe-
faultSettings%5D=1&g2_return=%2Fgallery%2Fmain.php%3Fg2_
itemId%3D15789&g2_returnName=photo HTTP/1.1" 200 6360 "-"
"Mozilla/5.0 (compatible; Googlebot/2.1; +>http://www.google.com/
bot.html)
Time taken: 9.102 seconds
```

As you will see, combined with the two additional views shown below, these results can be used to produce a ratio of failed to successful requests by day, across the period of months and years within the server logs.

```
--Unsuccessful server calls as a time series by year, month, and
day
Create VIEW FailedRequestsTimeSeriesByDay AS
SELECT yearmonthday, COUNT(yearmonthday) AS failedrequest_freq
FROM by_day
WHERE substr(status,1,1) IN('4','5')
GROUP BY yearmonthday
ORDER BY yearmonthday ASC;

--Successful server calls as a time series by year, month, and day
Create VIEW SuccessfulRequestsTimeSeriesByDay AS
```

```
SELECT yearmonthday, COUNT(yearmonthday) AS successfulrequest_freq
FROM by_day
WHERE substr(status,1,1) IN('1','2','3')
GROUP BY yearmonthday
ORDER BY yearmonthday ASC;
```

Finally, you will see these two views are joined in the query below, to produce the failed-to-successful request ratio by day.

```
--Calculate ratio of failed to successful requests by year, month,
and day
SELECT a.yearmonthday, a.failedrequest_freq / b.successfulrequest_
freq AS failratio
FROM FailedRequestsTimeSeriesByDay a
JOIN SuccessfulRequestsTimeSeriesByDay b
ON a.yearmonthday = b.yearmonthday
ORDER BY yearmonthday ASC;
```

We display the results for our request below.

```
yearmonthday failratio
20090720     0.023759608665269043
20090721     0.024037482175595846
20090722     0.029298848252172157
20090723     0.032535684298908484
20090724     0.045442359249329760
20090725     0.030345800988002825
20090726     0.031446540880503145
20090727     0.034940600978336830
20090728     0.031545741324921134
20090729     0.031383737517831670
20090730     0.035902851108764520
20090731     0.034519956850053934
20090801     0.024278676988036593
20090802     0.029702970297029700
20090803     0.031402651779483600
20090804     0.030692362598144184
20090805     0.039501779359430604
20090806     0.030526315789473683
20090807     0.037624180934263370
20090808     0.029632274187790075
20090809     0.029971791255289138
20090810     0.035639412997903560
20090811     0.036671368124118475
20090812     0.033497884344146690
20090813     0.030769230769230770
20090814     0.031578947368421054
20090815     0.031918625043844270
20090816     0.033645508151231360
20090817     0.029210241615578794
20090818     0.030576789437109102
```

```
20090819      0.033402922755741124
20090820      0.034220532319391636
20090821      0.032474408753971055
20090822      0.03897944720056697
20090823      0.029098651525904896
20090824      0.028070175438596492
20090825      0.02638058389025677
20090826      0.029650547123190964
20090827      0.029627047751829907
20090828      0.039628704034273474
20090829      0.035426166257453526
20090830      0.02492102492102492
20090831      0.032418952618453865
20090901      0.02949438202247191
20090902      0.032688927943760986
20090903      0.028690662493479395
20090904      0.029954719609892023
20090905      0.02907180385288967
20090906      0.031042901988140914
20090907      0.03449477351916376
20090908      0.035181236673773986
20090909      0.037141846480367884
20090910      0.03450679679330777
20090911      0.03566433566433566
20090912      0.031282952548330405
20090913      0.030218825981243487
20090914      0.03377437325905292
20090915      0.025804171085189113
20090916      0.030892051371051717
20090917      0.030978934324659233
20090918      0.028441011235955056
20090919      0.02912280701754386
20090920      0.027392510402219142
20090921      0.03273381294964029
20090922      0.031751570132588974
20090923      0.03167898627243928
20090924      0.03349964362081254
20090925      0.0420377627360171
20090926      0.03863716192483316
20090927      0.0328042328042328
20090928      0.040757954951734
20090929      0.030975008799718408
20090930      0.03368794326241135
20091001      0.028916929547844375
Time taken: 68.21 seconds
```

We can also export and analyze the report in a program, such as R, Excel, or SAS. Aggregating data into a time series is one way to turn large data into small data that can be analyzed with more conventional tools. Rerunning the last query with the INSERT OVERWRITE LOCAL DIRECTORY command exports the results for further analysis. We display the Hive input next. Most of the output was omitted, due to the size of the data. Prior to using this command, you should be aware that it will overwrite all files that already exist within your target folder. A good way to avoid overwriting your folder is to provide a new folder name at the end of the location address string—"FailedRequestsBy-Day." Also, one trade-off worth noting with views is that when calling a view in another query, the view query is rerun. This lengthens run times and increases the verbosity of the command line output.

```
hive> INSERT OVERWRITE LOCAL DIRECTORY '/mnt/hgfs/BigDataAnalytics/
Project1/FailedRequestsByDay'
    > SELECT a.yearmonthday
    > ,a.failedrequest_freq / b.successfulrequest_freq AS failratio
    > FROM FailedRequestsTimeSeriesByDay a
    > JOIN SuccessfulRequestsTimeSeriesByDay b
    > ON a.yearmonthday = b.yearmonthday
    > ORDER BY yearmonthday ASC;
Total MapReduce jobs = 6
Launching Job 1 out of 6
Number of reduce tasks not specified. Estimated from input data
size: 1
...
Total MapReduce CPU Time Spent: 18 seconds 800 msec
OK
```

As you will see, the output file is easily imported into R. We can even specify the standard delimiter used in Hive. This delimiter, which appears as ^A in graphical form, is actually quite useful. Unlike a comma or other typical delimiters, it is highly unlikely that most data will include Hive's standard delimiter, which is, of course, why the developers of Hive chose to use this delimiter.

Next, the code snippet below shows some R code used to import the data and perform a simple control limits test to see what days had ratios that exceed a threshold. The threshold is defined as the average plus two times the standard deviation.

```
> rm(list=ls()) #Remove any objects
>
> library(fBasics)
>
> #Import failed requests file, using standard delimeter in Hive
> failedRequests <- read.table("FailedRequestsByDay.txt",sep="")
>
> #Add column headings
> colnames(failedRequests) <- c("Date","FailedRequestsRatio")
> stdev <- sd(failedRequests$FailedRequestsRatio) #calculate the
standard deviation
```

```
> avg <- mean(failedRequests$FailedRequestsRatio) #calculate the
average
> avgPlus2Stdev <- avg + 2*stdev #mean plus 2 standard deviations
>
> #Identify the days that had failed requests in excess of 2X the
standard deviation
> failedRequests[failedRequests[,2]>avgPlus2Stdev,]
   Date     FailedRequestsRatio
5  20090724  0.04544236
68 20090925  0.04203776
71 20090928  0.04075795
>
> #Produce a plot and save it as a PDF
> pdf("PlotOfFailedRequestRatioSeries.pdf")
> plot(failedRequests[,2],type='l',main="Ratio of Failed Server
Requests to Successful Requests by Day"
+ ,xlab="Day",ylab="Ratio of Failed Requests to Successful Requests")
> lines(rep(avg,length(failedRequests[,2])))
> lines(rep(avgPlus2Stdev,length(failedRequests[,2])),lty=2)
> legend("topright",c("Average","2 X Standard Devia-
tion"),lty=c(1,2))
> dev.off()
null device 1
>
> #Create autocorrelation plot to test for seasonality or other
autocorrelation effects
> pdf("FaileRequestsAutoCorrelation.pdf")
> acfPlot(failedRequests[,2],lag.max=60)
> dev.off()
null device 1
```

In the excerpted output below, we can see that there were three occurrences that exceeded the threshold: July 24, 2009; September 25, 2009; and September 28, 2009.

```
   Date     FailedRequestsRatio
5  20090724 0.04544236
68 20090925 0.04203776
71 20090928 0.04075795
```

The control plot is shown below (Figure 3.1).

Since it is possible that some of the variation could be due to seasonality or other causes, we need to perform an analysis of autocorrelation with the acfPlot() function, as part of the "fBasics" package. You will see that the resulting plot, however, gives no indication of seasonal effects. The tallest and only statistically significant bar in the graph is at the zero lag point on the x-axis. Any bars appearing above the dotted line would have indicated a statistically significant autocorrelation effect at that lag point (Figure 3.2).

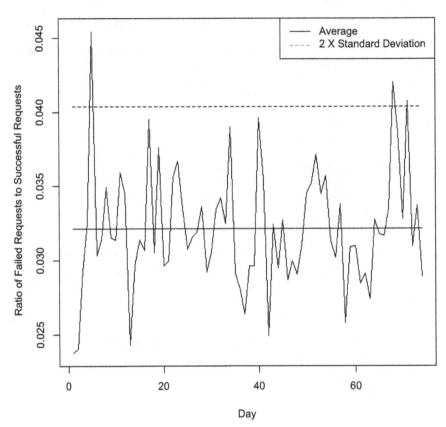

FIGURE 3.1

Ratio of failed server requests to successful requests by day.

We merely suggest this as a starting point to demonstrate a means of organizing, aggregating, and sorting the time field. Further parsing could also be done on hours, minutes, and seconds as well. The Hive output can be used in conjunction with other tools to provide visualizations of the data, as well as to perform analysis that is generally unavailable within the Hadoop, MapReduce environment.

Hive for Producing Analytical Data Sets

We use the "statusgroupings" view, which was reviewed toward the beginning of this document, to produce an analytical data set that could be useful for analysis in other tools. As an example, a logistic regression was run to determine if we could find any patterns among the variables that might be predictive of request failure or success (as indicated by the status codes). However, there are too many categorical variables across too many dimensions to produce any

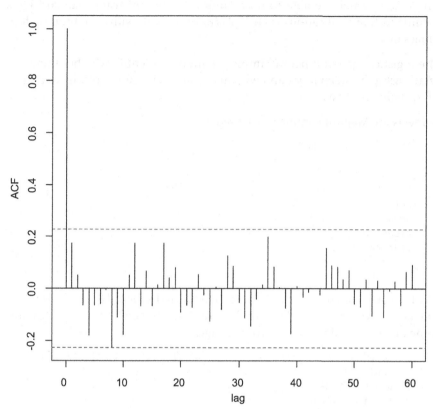

SS.1

FIGURE 3.2
Testing for autocorrelation effects in the time series, such as seasonality.

apparently meaningful results. We have reproduced the method and results here, mainly as an exercise.

We created the analytical data set by using the following Hive code, which calls the view and exports the data to a local directory.

```
INSERT OVERWRITE LOCAL DIRECTORY '/mnt/hgfs/BigDataAnalytics/Proj-
ect1/ApacheLog'
SELECT * FROM statusgroupings;
```

We ran the logistic regression by using Mahout. While Hive's standard delim-iter of "^A" can be useful for a number of data sets and analysis tools (such as R), Mahout prefers data in traditional CSV format, with a comma. You may be able to use the Hive command "set hive.io.output.fileformat = CSVTextFile" prior to running the export snippet above. However, this does not seem to always work for everyone, perhaps depending upon your environment. Barring this, you may be able to do a "find and replace" using standard Unix command line applications such as AWK, or SED, or with an editor, such as Emacs or Vi.

The logistic regression below simply attempts to identify whether there is a relationship between hosts and whether or not they tend to produce successful or failed requests.

Below is the Mahout command we used.

```
/usr/bin/mahout trainlogistic \
--input statusgroupings.csv \
--output ./model \
--target failedaccess \
--categories 2 \
--predictors host \
--types word \
--features 50 \
--passes 20 \
--rate 50
```

The full command line output is far too lengthy to list here. However, segments of it are shown below. Incidentally, the term "failedaccess" is the variable name to be predicted and is not an error message.

```
[cloudera@localhost Project1]$ /usr/bin/mahout trainlogistic \
> --input statusgroupings.csv \
> --output ./model \
> --target failedaccess \
> --categories 2 \
> --predictors host identity user \
> --types word \
> --features 50 \
> --passes 20 \
> --rate 50
MAHOUT_LOCAL is not set; adding HADOOP_CONF_DIR to classpath.
Running on hadoop, using /usr/lib/hadoop/bin/hadoop and HADOOP_
CONF_DIR=/etc/hadoop/conf
MAHOUT-JOB: /usr/lib/mahout/mahout-examples-0.7-cdh4.2.0-job.jar
50
failedaccess ~ -3.757*Intercept Term + -19.927*host=112.200.11.174
+ -18.807*host=112.200.200.192 + ...
...
Intercept Term -3.75710
host=112.200.11.174 -19.92741
host=112.200.200.192 -18.80668
host=112.202.3.173 -0.08841
host=112.202.43.173 1.03845
host=114.111.36.26 0.33822
```

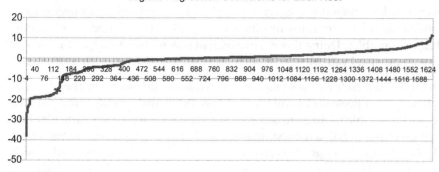

FIGURE 3.3

Logistic regression coefficients for each host.

```
host=114.127.246.36 3.49805
host=114.200.199.144 0.47374
host=114.39.145.56 -3.32575
...
13/05/07 18:28:30 INFO driver.MahoutDriver: Program took 70195 ms
(Minutes: 1.1699166666666667)
```

Next we copy the long list of hosts and their respective coefficients into a spreadsheet program for some quick visualization. The graph in figure 3.3 shows how a few top hosts tend to drive a negative prediction of a request failure. In other words, some hosts are strongly associated with consistent requests with no failures. On the right side of the graph, the gradual slope suggests less predictive potential for hosts that can be associated with failed requests. The numbers on the x-axis are index numbers, with one number per host.

These results are not that surprising, given that we already know that this data set does not exhibit strong attack patterns, aside from a few isolated attack cases that were added to it. If we had a data set containing a series of events leading up to an attack, there might, indeed, be some hosts that could be characterized by failed requests. However, a sorted list of top hosts by failed requests, as was produced earlier, would also reveal this. If we had a larger number of positively identified breaches, logistic regression and other classifiers might prove more useful. Nevertheless, this exercise shows how Hive is useful for producing data sets suitable for analysis with other tools, such as Mahout (Figure 3.3).

ANOTHER POTENTIAL ANALYTICAL DATA SET: UNSTACKED STATUS CODES

You will see some analytical tools and methods requiring categories to be unstacked. That is, each category within a column must be converted into its own separate column. Each new category column contains a numeral one for every row for which the category applies and a zero otherwise. Converting categorical data into columns in this way is sometimes referred to as creating dummy variables. Doing this is a convenient way to turn a categorical variable into a numerical variable.

The following code unstacks the category codes in this manner. The idea here is that each of these status codes could have predictive potential. For instance, we might be able to do a cross-correlation over time to see if a particular host had a number of failed requests that are predictive of a string of successes later. Or, failed requests might also precede large file sizes being transferred as well. Following is Hive code that could be a starting point for such an analysis.

```
--Unstack status codes into individual columns, create date fields,
and show all other columns as well

CREATE VIEW IF NOT EXISTS unstacked_status_codes AS
SELECT host, identity, user, time, CASE substr(time,5,3)
WHEN 'Jan' THEN '01'
WHEN 'Feb' THEN '02'
WHEN 'Mar' THEN '03'
WHEN 'Apr' THEN '04'
WHEN 'May' THEN '05'
WHEN 'Jun' THEN '06'
WHEN 'Jul' THEN '07'
WHEN 'Aug' THEN '08'
WHEN 'Sep' THEN '09'
WHEN 'Oct' THEN '10'
WHEN 'Nov' THEN '11'
WHEN 'Dec' THEN '12'
ELSE '00'
END
AS month, substr(time,9,4) AS year, concat(substr(time,9,4), CASE
substr(time,5,3) WHEN 'Jan' THEN '01'
WHEN 'Feb' THEN '02'
WHEN 'Mar' THEN '03'
WHEN 'Apr' THEN '04'
WHEN 'May' THEN '05'
WHEN 'Jun' THEN '06'
WHEN 'Jul' THEN '07'
WHEN 'Aug' THEN '08'
WHEN 'Sep' THEN '09'
WHEN 'Oct' THEN '10'
WHEN 'Nov' THEN '11'
WHEN 'Dec' THEN '12'
ELSE '00'
END) AS yearmonth, concat(CASE substr(time,5,3)
WHEN 'Jan' THEN '01'
WHEN 'Feb' THEN '02'
```

```
WHEN 'Mar' THEN '03'
WHEN 'Apr' THEN '04'
WHEN 'May' THEN '05'
WHEN 'Jun' THEN '06'
WHEN 'Jul' THEN '07'
WHEN 'Aug' THEN '08'
WHEN 'Sep' THEN '09'
WHEN 'Oct' THEN '10'
WHEN 'Nov' THEN '11'
WHEN 'Dec' THEN '12'
ELSE '00'
END,substr(time,2,2)) AS monthday, request, CASE status WHEN '100'
THEN 1 ELSE 0 END AS 100Continue, CASE status WHEN '101' THEN 1
ELSE 0 END AS 101SwitchingProtocols, CASE status WHEN '102' THEN 1
ELSE 0 END AS 102Processing, CASE status WHEN '200' THEN 1 ELSE 0
END AS 200OK, CASE status WHEN '201' THEN 1 ELSE 0 END AS 201Cre-
ated, CASE status WHEN '202' THEN 1 ELSE 0 END AS 202Accepted, CASE
status WHEN '203' THEN 1 ELSE 0 END AS 203NonAuthoritativeInforma-
tion, CASE status WHEN '204' THEN 1 ELSE 0 END AS 204NoContent, CASE
status WHEN '205' THEN 1 ELSE 0 END AS 205ResetContent, CASE status
WHEN '206' THEN 1 ELSE 0 END AS 206PartialContent, CASE status WHEN
'207' THEN 1 ELSE 0 END AS 207MultiStatus, CASE status WHEN '208'
THEN 1 ELSE 0 END AS 208AlreadyReported, CASE status WHEN '226' THEN
1 ELSE 0 END AS 226IMUsed, CASE status WHEN '300' THEN 1 ELSE 0 END
AS 300MultipleChoices, CASE status WHEN '301' THEN 1 ELSE 0 END AS
301MovedPermanently, CASE status WHEN '302' THEN 1 ELSE 0 END AS
302Found, CASE status WHEN '303' THEN 1 ELSE 0 END AS 303SeeOther,
CASE status WHEN '304' THEN 1 ELSE 0 END AS 304NotModified, CASE
status WHEN '305' THEN 1 ELSE 0 END AS 305UseProxy, CASE status WHEN
'306' THEN 1 ELSE 0 END AS 306SwitchProxy, CASE status WHEN '307'
THEN 1 ELSE 0 END AS 307TemporaryRedirect, CASE status WHEN '308'
THEN 1 ELSE 0 END AS 308PermanentRedirect, CASE status WHEN '400'
THEN 1 ELSE 0 END AS 400BadRequest, CASE status WHEN '401' THEN 1
ELSE 0 END AS 401Unauthorized, CASE status WHEN '402' THEN 1 ELSE 0
END AS 402PaymentRequired, CASE status WHEN '403' THEN 1 ELSE 0 END
AS 403Forbidden, CASE status WHEN '404' THEN 1 ELSE 0 END AS 404Not-
Found, CASE status WHEN '405' THEN 1 ELSE 0 END AS 405MethodNotAl-
lowed, CASE status WHEN '406' THEN 1 ELSE 0 END AS 406NotAcceptable,
CASE status WHEN '407' THEN 1 ELSE 0 END AS 407ProxyAuthentication-
Required, CASE status WHEN '408' THEN 1 ELSE 0 END AS 408RequestTim-
eout, CASE status WHEN '409' THEN 1 ELSE 0 END AS 409Conflict, CASE
status WHEN '410' THEN 1 ELSE 0 END AS 410Gone, CASE status WHEN
'411' THEN 1 ELSE 0 END AS 411LengthRequired, CASE status WHEN '412'
THEN 1 ELSE 0 END AS 412PreconditionFailed, CASE status WHEN '413'
THEN 1 ELSE 0 END AS 413RequestEntityTooLarge, CASE status WHEN
'414' THEN 1 ELSE 0 END AS 414RequestUriTooLong, CASE status WHEN
'415' THEN 1 ELSE 0 END AS 415UnsupportedMediaType, CASE status WHEN
'416' THEN 1 ELSE 0 END AS 416RequestedRangeNotSatisfiable, CASE
status WHEN '417' THEN 1 ELSE 0 END AS 417ExpectationFailed, CASE
```

```
status WHEN '418' THEN 1 ELSE 0 END AS 418ImATeapot, CASE status
WHEN '420' THEN 1 ELSE 0 END AS 420EnhanceYourCalm, CASE status WHEN
'422' THEN 1 ELSE 0 END AS 422UnprocessableEntity, CASE status WHEN
'423' THEN 1 ELSE 0 END AS 423Locked, CASE status WHEN '424' THEN
1 ELSE 0 END AS 424FailedDependency, CASE status WHEN '424' THEN 1
ELSE 0 END AS 424MethodFailure, CASE status WHEN '425' THEN 1 ELSE
0 END AS 425UnorderedCollection, CASE status WHEN '426' THEN 1 ELSE
0 END AS 426UpgradeRequired, CASE status WHEN '428' THEN 1 ELSE 0
END AS 428PreconditionRequired, CASE status WHEN '429' THEN 1 ELSE
0 END AS 429TooManyRequests, CASE status WHEN '431' THEN 1 ELSE 0
END AS 431RequestHeaderFieldsTooLarge, CASE status WHEN '444' THEN
1 ELSE 0 END AS 444NoResponse, CASE status WHEN '449' THEN 1 ELSE
0 END AS 449RetryWith, CASE status WHEN '450' THEN 1 ELSE 0 END AS
450BlockedByWindowsParentalControls, CASE status WHEN '451' THEN 1
ELSE 0 END AS 451UnavailableForLegalReasonsOrRedirect, CASE sta-
tus WHEN '494' THEN 1 ELSE 0 END AS 494RequestHeaderTooLarge, CASE
status WHEN '495' THEN 1 ELSE 0 END AS 495CertError, CASE status
WHEN '496' THEN 1 ELSE 0 END AS 496NoCert, CASE status WHEN '497'
THEN 1 ELSE 0 END AS 497HttpToHttps, CASE status WHEN '499' THEN 1
ELSE 0 END AS 499ClientClosedRequest, CASE status WHEN '500' THEN
1 ELSE 0 END AS 500InternalServerError, CASE status WHEN '501' THEN
1 ELSE 0 END AS 501NotImplemented, CASE status WHEN '502' THEN 1
ELSE 0 END AS 502BadGateway, CASE status WHEN '503' THEN 1 ELSE 0
END AS 503ServiceUnavailable, CASE status WHEN '504' THEN 1 ELSE 0
END AS 504GatewayTimeout, CASE status WHEN '505' THEN 1 ELSE 0 END
AS 505HttpVersionNotSupported, CASE status WHEN '506' THEN 1 ELSE 0
END AS 506VariantAlsoNegotiates, CASE status WHEN '507' THEN 1 ELSE
0 END AS 507InsufficientStorage, CASE status WHEN '508' THEN 1 ELSE
0 END AS 508LoopDetected, CASE status WHEN '509' THEN 1 ELSE 0 END
AS 509BandwidthLimitExceeded, CASE status WHEN '510' THEN 1 ELSE 0
END AS 510NotExtended, CASE status WHEN '511' THEN 1 ELSE 0 END AS
511NetworkAuthenticationRequired, CASE status WHEN '598' THEN 1 ELSE
0 END AS 598NetworkReadTimeoutError, CASE status WHEN '599' THEN 1
ELSE 0 END AS 599NetworkConnectTimeoutError, size, referer, agent
FROM apachelog;
```

As you will see, the output from creating the view indicates that all of these variables were created.

```
OK
host identity user time month year yearmonth monthday
    request 100continue 101switchingprotocols
    102processing 200ok 201created 202accepted
    203nonauthoritativeinformation 204nocontent
    205resetcontent 206partialcontent 207multistatus
    208alreadyreported 226imused 300multiplechoices
    301movedpermanently 302found 303seeother 304notmodified
    305useproxy 306switchproxy 307temporaryredirect
    308permanentredirect 400badrequest 401unauthorized
    402paymentrequired 403forbidden 404notfound
```

```
405methodnotallowed 406notacceptable
407proxyauthenticationrequired 408requesttimeout
409conflict 410gone 411lengthrequired
412preconditionfailed 413requestentitytoolarge
414requesturitoolong 415unsupportedmediatype
416requestedrangenotsatisfiable 417expectationfailed
418imateapot 420enhanceyourcalm 422unprocessableentity
423locked 424faileddependency 424methodfailure
425unorderedcollection 426upgraderequired
428preconditionrequired 429toomanyrequests
431requestheaderfieldstoolarge 444noresponse
449retrywith 450blockedbywindowsparentalcontrols
451unavailableforlegalreasonsorredirect
494requestheadertoolarge 495certerror 496nocert
497httptohttps 499clientclosedrequest
500internalservererror 501notimplemented 502badgateway
503serviceunavailable 504gatewaytimeout
505httpversionnotsupported 506variantalsonegotiates
507insufficientstorage 508loopdetected
509bandwidthlimitexceeded 510notextended
511networkauthenticationrequired
598networkreadtimeouterror
599networkconnecttimeouterrorsize referer agent
Time taken: 2.128 seconds
```

We then took the results and sent it as an output to a text file so that it can be available for further analysis with external tools, presuming you, as the analyst, have enough memory on your machine. If not, then further aggregation with Hive would be desirable, perhaps grouping counts of all the status codes by day. We used the following command to export the file.

```
INSERT OVERWRITE LOCAL DIRECTORY '/mnt/hgfs/BigDataAnalytics/Proj-
ect1/UnstackedStatusCodes'
SELECT count()
FROM unstacked_status_codes;
```

We have provided the first row of the output below. You will see that although this output may look like a table, it is a single, wide row that is wrapped.

```
66.249.67.3 - - [20/Jul/2009:20:12:22 -0700] 07 2009 200907
0720 "GET /gallery/main.php?g2_controller=exif.SwitchDetailM-
ode&g2_mode=detailed&g2_return=%2Fgallery%2Fmain.php%3Fg2_
itemId%3D15741&g2_returnName=photo HTTP/1.1" 0 0 0 0 0 0 0 0 0
0 0 0 0 1 0 0 0 0 0 0 0 0 0 0 0 0 0 0 00 0 0 0 0 0 0 0 0 0
0 0 0 0 0 00 0 0 0 0 0 0 0 0 0 0 0 0 0 0 0 00 0 0 0 0 0 5 "-"
"Mozilla/5.0 (compatible; Googlebot/2.1; +>http://www.google.com/
bot.html)
```

We should see only a single numeral one, with all other status categories being zero. Since that is what we find, it appears our query was successful.

OTHER APPLICABLE SECURITY AREAS AND SCENARIOS

Although these examples involved server logs, the same methods can be applied to forensic analysis of data from other systems sources as well. For instance, data collected on network traffic, such as from router log files, can also accumulate in very large amounts. Big data tools and analysis methods can similarly prove useful for these scenarios as well.

One of the main challenges in analyzing other kinds of log files is parsing all the text data. There is an enormous variety of file formats that an analyst could encounter. Generally, these files are parsed using regular expressions, such as shown at the beginning of this chapter. However, writing regular expressions is notoriously challenging and generally requires a significant amount of patience, and trial-and-error attempts. Do not give up. There are plenty of examples for most common server log types, which are available from your favorite Web search engine. You can start out with an example and tweak it to adapt it to your specific format. It is also helpful to have a regular expression editing tool. There are many of these to choose from on the Internet and quite a few of them are free. One such favorite among many analysts is www.regexr.com.

Another option to writing regular expressions from scratch is to try a parsing tool. A popular tool for running on Windows operating systems is Log Parser by Microsoft. Do not expect a nice graphical interface though, as it is command line based. Reviewing all the possible parsing tools is beyond the scope of this book. But, there are a number of them available and new ones continue to be developed.

Of course, log files are not the only sources of data available for analysis. For example, e-mail and network traffic sniffers can also be valuable sources of security-related data. Many of the same techniques can be applied as with server logs. For instance, e-mail messages have various components that can be parsed, stored, and queried, such as the recipient, sender, date stamp, and so on. The same can be said of the output from network sniffers. However, e-mail messages tend to have larger amounts of unstructured data within the body section, and this requires different methods of analysis than what we have discussed in this chapter. Text mining techniques are particularly useful for unstructured data. We will cover some text mining techniques in Chapter 6.

SUMMARY

Hive provides a very useful framework for analyzing large amounts of server log data. As attack vectors are so varied, a flexible tool that enables drilldowns and ad hoc analysis on the fly is very useful. However, it can also be useful to have a collection of queries and methods for analyzing common attack vectors as a starting point. We hope that the ideas offered here may serve as a catalyst for further creativity and research into this topic.

FURTHER READING

Analyze Log Data with Apache Hive, Windows PowerShell, and Amazon EMR: Articles & Tutorials: Amazon Web Services. http://aws.amazon.com/articles/3681655242374956 (accessed 17.04.13.).

Apache Log Analysis with Hadoop, Hive and HBase. https://gist.github.com/emk/1556097 (accessed 17.04.13.).

Analyze Log Data with Apache Hive, Windows PowerShell, and Amazon EMR: Articles & Tutorials: Amazon Web Services. http://aws.amazon.com/articles/3681655242374956 (accessed 06.05.13.).

Analyzing Apache Logs with Hadoop Map/Reduce. | Rajvish. http://rajvish.wordpress.com/2012/04/30/analyzing-apache-logs-with-hadoop-mapreduce/ (accessed 17.04.13.).

Apache Log Analysis with Hadoop, Hive and HBase. https://gist.github.com/emk/1556097 (accessed 17.04.13.).

Apache Log Analysis Using Pig: Articles & Tutorials: Amazon Web Services. http://aws.amazon.com/code/Elastic-MapReduce/2728 (accessed 17.04.13.).

Blind-sqli-regexp-attack.pdf. http://www.ihteam.net/papers/blind-sqli-regexp-attack.pdf (accessed 07.05.13.).

Devi, T. Hive and Hadoop for Data Analytics on Large Web Logs. May 8, 2012. http://www.devx.com/Java/Article/48100.

Exploring Apache Log Files Using Hive and Hadoop | Johnandcailin. http://www.johnandcailin.com/blog/cailin/exploring-apache-log-files-using-hive-and-hadoop (accessed 17.04.13.).

Fingerprinting Port80 Attacks: A Look into Web Server, and Web Application Attack Signatures: Part Two. http://www.cgisecurity.com/fingerprinting-port80-attacks-a-look-into-web-server-and-web-application-attack-signatures-part-two.html (accessed 08.05.13.).

Googlebot Makes an Appearance in Web Analytics Reports. http://searchengineland.com/is-googlebot-skewing-google-analytics-data-22313 (accessed 05.05.13.).

[#HIVE-662] Add a Method to Parse Apache Weblogs – ASF JIRA. https://issues.apache.org/jira/browse/HIVE-662 (accessed 17.04.13.).

IBM Security Intelligence with Big Data. http://www-03.ibm.com/security/solution/intelligence-big-data/ (accessed 20.04.13.).

Intro to Mahout – DC Hadoop. http://www.slideshare.net/gsingers/intro-to-mahout-dc-hadoop (accessed 06.05.13.).

Kick Start Hadoop: Analyzing Apache Logs with Pig. http://kickstarthadoop.blogspot.com/2011/06/analyzing-apache-logs-with-pig.html (accessed 17.04.13.).

LAthesis.pdf - Fry_MASc_F2011.pdf. http://spectrum.library.concordia.ca/7769/1/Fry_MASc_F2011.pdf (accessed 04.05.13.).

Log Files – Apache HTTP Server. http://httpd.apache.org/docs/current/logs.html#accesslog (accessed 25.04.13.).

Mod_log_config – Apache HTTP Server. http://httpd.apache.org/docs/2.0/mod/mod_log_config.html (accessed 17.04.13.).

New Tab. (accessed 07.05.13.) about:newtab.

Parsing Logs with Apache Pig and Elastic MapReduce: Articles & Tutorials: Amazon Web Services. http://aws.amazon.com/articles/2729 (accessed 22.04.13.).

Reading the Log Files – Apache. http://www.devshed.com/c/a/Apache/Logging-in-Apache/2/ (accessed 24.04.13.).

Recommender Documentation. https://cwiki.apache.org/MAHOUT/recommender-documentation. html (accessed 06.05.13.).

SQL Injection Cheat Sheet. http://ferruh.mavituna.com/sql-injection-cheatsheet-oku/ (accessed 07.05.13.).

Talabis, Ryan. Attack Samples, Apache Server Log Entries with Examples of Attacks and Security Breaches. April 25, 2013.

Tutorial. https://cwiki.apache.org/Hive/tutorial.html#Tutorial-Builtinoperators (accessed 05.05.13.).

User Agent – Wikipedia, the Free Encyclopedia. https://en.wikipedia.org/wiki/User_agent (accessed 07.04.13.).

Using Grepexe for Forensic Log Parsing and Analysis on Windows Server and IIS – IIS – Sysadmins of the North. http://www.saotn.org/using-grep-exe-for-forensic-log-parsing-and-analysis-on-windows-server-iis/ (accessed 04.05.13.).

Using Hive for Weblog Analysis | Digital Daaroo – by Saurabh Nanda. http://www.saurabhnanda. com/2009/07/using-hive-for-weblog-analysis.html (accessed 17.04.13.).

Using Versioning – Amazon Simple Storage Service. http://docs.aws.amazon.com/AmazonS3/ latest/dev/Versioning.html (accessed 22.02.13.).

## CHAPTER 4

Simulations and Security Processes

INFORMATION IN THIS CHAPTER:

- Simulations and security processes
  - Scenarios and challenges in security decisions-making and process implementation
  - Use of simulations in "what-if" security scenarios and strategic decision-making
  - Case study: step-by-step guide on how to create a simulation model based on real-life statistics and processes.

SIMULATION

The primary tool that we will be using in this chapter about simulations is Arena, which is commercial software developed by Rockwell Automation. Arena is a powerful modeling and simulation software allowing a user to model and run simulation experiments. We will be using a fully functioning perpetual evaluation version, which is available for study and download at (http://www.arenasimulation.com/Tools_Resources_Download_Arena.aspx).

Let us get started with simulations. Since Arena is a Windows desktop application, when you start using the program, you will see three regions on the main Arena window. Let us familiarize you with the three regions:

- At the left-hand side of the main window, you will find the Project bar containing three tabs: basic process, report and navigate panel. In the Project bar, you will also find various "Arena modules" to be used when building a simulation model. We will discuss more about Arena modules in the latter part of this section.
- At the right-hand side, you will find the Model window flowchart view to be the largest part of your screen because it is your workspace where you will create models. You will be creating graphical models using flowcharts, images, animations, and other drawn elements.

- At the bottom part of the flowchart view, you will find the Model window spreadsheet view, which presents all the data associated with the model.

This chapter will provide a high-level overview of creating simulations in Arena. There are three main steps to making a simulation in Arena:

1. Design and create a model,
2. Add data and parameters to a model,
3. Run a simulation, and
4. Analyze a simulation.

Designing and Creating a Model

Before we start in Arena, we first need to create a "conceptual model" for a scenario we will simulate. A conceptual model is how you think a process should work—this could be anything from you just drawing it out on a piece of paper or just thinking about it.

Once you have a conceptual model, the next step is to build the model in the workspace using the "modules" in Arena. Modules are the building blocks of a model. There are two kinds of modules: the flowchart modules and the data modules.

The flowchart modules illustrate the logic of your simulation. Some common flowchart modules found in the "Basic Process" tab of the Project bar are the following elements: CREATE, PROCESS, DECIDE, DISPOSE, BATCH, SEPARATE, and ASSIGN and RECORD. To use these modules, you simply drag the flowchart module needed into the model and then you connect the modules together in the Model window flowchart view. For example, if I were to create our conceptual model of the IT service desk ticket queue, it would look like this (Figure 4.1).

As you see in our figure, we used the CREATE, PROCESS, and a DISPOSE modules to illustrate the logic of the queue. Once service desk tickets are created by the IT Department (CREATE module), it is processed by IT Department (PROCESS module), and it is closed by IT Department (DISPOSE module). A bit confused? Rest assured, we have a whole chapter about this and it will get clearer as we take you step by step through an actual scenario.

For now, we are starting with a three-process scenario to get you thinking about simulation. This quick start model is provided on the companion site for download. For now, just think of it as creating a flowchart of your scenario. If you have used Microsoft Visio before, you will be right at home.

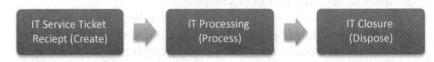

FIGURE 4.1
IT service desk process.

Adding Data and Parameters to the Model

After creating the flowchart, the next step is to add data to each of the flowchart modules. You may assign the values for each module by double clicking on the modules in the model, which will open up a small dialog window. For example, for the CREATE module, let us say tickets arrive at an average of five per hour. You would enter that value directly into the CREATE module. Additionally, let us say tickets are processed and resolved at an average rate of 30 min. You would assign this value into your PROCESS module. We will provide you with a more detailed walk-through on how to do this later in this chapter.

Running the Simulation

After the model is complete, all you need to do is to select "Go" from the Run menu or press F5. There are other parameters that you may want to set up before running the simulation, such as the replication parameters where you can set the simulation period. But for the purpose of this quick introduction, we will just run the simulation.

Analyzing the Simulation

Arena provides a variety of reports so that you may analyze the simulation. You access the Reports panel from the Project bar.

CASE STUDY

There are a lot of interesting uses for simulations in security. One of them is evaluating the effect of security controls or mechanisms in your enterprise that otherwise would be difficult to recreate. For this chapter, let us put ourselves in the position of an Information Security Officer, who needs to evaluate different antivirus (AV) e-mail security gateway offerings. One of the main things you will be concerned about is performance of the e-mail gateway device. Since the device will be sitting in-line and processing network traffic, you would want to make sure that the e-mail gateway is able to handle the volume of e-mails coming into your organization. Since this device will also sit in front of your e-mail server, there is no convenient way to test how the different e-mail security gateways will perform. This is where simulations come into play. Simulations give us a way to predict how a certain scenario or situation will play out based on available data. Of course, it will not be the same as testing the real thing, but it will at least provide us an estimate so that we can make an informed decision (Table 4.1).

One of the first things we need for a simulation is data. Fortunately, in our scenario, a vendor (hereafter referred to as Vendor 1) provided us with a data set comparing its e-mail security gateway solution with products from other vendors (hereafter referred to as Vendor 2 and Vendor 3). You can download this data set from the book's website. Next, we will explain how this data set will be used in our scenario.

Table 4.1 Vendor Scenario Data

	Vendor 1	Vendor 2	Vendor 3
Average (s)	0.177271963	0.669560187	0.569069159
Test data (s)	0.0077	0.0119	0.5994
	0.0018	0.0201	0.5269
	0.0101	3.4405	0.4258
	0.0144	0.0701	0.5109
	0.0134	0.02	0.5619
	0.006	0.0119	0.5017
	0.1103	0.0012	0.4382
	0.0113	0.013	0.4346
	0.0116	0.0161	0.4988
	0.0185	0.0157	0.49
	0.0021	0.2894	0.4843
	0.0088	0.0089	0.4602
	0.0051	0.0056	0.4431
	0.0061	0.0067	1.4135
	0.0106	0.0206	0.4199
	0.0064	0.221	0.4332
	0.01	0.025	0.4162
	0.0128	3.067	0.4386
	0.0113	1.098	0.4342
	0.01	0.0158	0.4309
	0.0058	1.145	0.4146
	0.0023	0.112	0.4392
	0.0126	0.0146	0.4678
	0.0128	0.0098	0.4608
	0.006	0.0201	0.4689
	0.0064	0.0139	0.481
	0.0088	0.0066	0.4449
	0.011	1.945	0.4312
	0.0142	0.8112	0.453
	0.0058	0.855	1.2839
	0.0062	0.874	0.445
	0.0063	1.589	0.4275
	0.014	0.0203	0.4517
	0.0946	0.89	1.092
	0.0011	0.0112	0.5119
	0.0073	2.547	0.5966
	0.0089	3.4003	1.2248
	0.0111	2.3314	0.4345
	0.0081	0.0158	0.5527

Table 4.1 Vendor Scenario Data *Continued*

	Vendor 1	Vendor 2	Vendor 3
	0.0114	0.0144	0.4991
	0.0096	0.0204	0.4213
	0.6305	0.0061	1.3264
	0.0113	0.0105	0.4312
	0.0059	2.578	0.4246
	0.0102	0.95	0.4422
	0.065	0.721	1.4509
	0.0063	3.3614	0.478
	0.0189	0.3078	0.4121
	0.9503	3.3444	1.1532
	0.0236	0.0103	0.4589
	0.0094	0.00254	0.4124
	0.0076	1.067	0.5074
	0.0057	0.905	0.4509
	1.0007	3.4747	0.4639
	0.0061	0.0205	0.4729
	0.0113	0.013	0.4343
	0.0094	0.0018	0.4359
	0.0061	0.0101	0.4761
	0.0088	1.345	0.4594
	0.0054	0.0936	0.6192
	0.9407	3.7085	1.1916
	12.2007	3.4655	0.5122
	0.0035	1.523	0.4097
	0.0028	0.0202	0.4422
	0.0042	0.0147	0.4585
	0.083	0.9678	1.282
	0.0009	0.0059	1.4524
	0.0078	0.0211	0.5503
	0.0357	0.0496	0.7331
	0.0068	0.016	0.4823
	0.0107	0.0177	0.4378
	0.0128	1.8678	0.4388
	0.0113	0.013	0.4349
	0.9457	0.812	0.9953
	0.0109	0.0071	0.4457
	0.0181	1.78	0.4099
	0.0099	0.0102	0.4278
	0.0066	0.832	0.4231
	0.0111	0.0127	0.4346
	0.0108	0.0144	0.4988

Continued...

Table 4.1 Vendor Scenario Data *Continued*

	Vendor 1	Vendor 2	Vendor 3
	0.0159	0.0026	1.4738
	0.0155	0.0772	0.4918
	0.0113	0.0136	0.4157
	0.0057	0.0101	0.4327
	0.0064	0.0125	0.5496
	0.0126	0.0146	0.4308
	0.0171	0.042	0.4525
	0.0038	0.1454	0.6053
	0.0059	1.89	0.4243
	0.0043	0.0407	0.7431
	0.0066	0.8901	0.4764
	0.0069	0.8542	0.4635
	0.01	0.0059	0.522
	0.0064	1.956	0.4802
	0.0119	1.993	0.4333
	0.0113	1.432	0.4343
	0.0111	0.0127	0.4347
	0.0064	0.0125	0.5521
	0.065	0.711	1.2924
	0.0912	0.0056	0.5121
	0.0059	0.0107	0.4661
	0.0125	0.0124	0.4177
	0.0113	0.013	0.4157
	0.8998	1.9081	0.4626
	0.0059	0.0102	0.4304
	0.0184	1.145	0.4216
	0.0099	0.0144	0.5201

Table 4.2 Vendor Processing Time - Overall Performance

	Average Processing
Vendor 1	0.177271963
Vendor 2	0.669560187
Vendor 3	0.569069159

Vendor 1 ran malicious e-mails through its e-mail security gateway and computed how fast the gateways processed the malicious e-mails (e.g., how fast the malicious e-mails were detected). Since Vendor 1 provided the data, as expected in terms of average processing times, Vendor 1 had an extremely short processing time (Table 4.2).

You may be asking yourself, how do we validate these numbers? Typically you would just take this data at face value and accept these numbers. However, what if you wanted to dive deeper to see if these are actually accurate for your organization's situation? This is where the fun part starts because we can do this through simulation. Let us dive into Arena!

First off, let us deconstruct our scenario. We need three components to start our simulation:

1. First, we need to create the e-mails;
2. Second, we need to create the 'e-mail security gateway' to process these e-mails; and
3. Third, we need to create the inboxes that will receive the e-mails.

Fortunately, creating all of these components is fairly easy to do in Arena. Let us start first by creating a stream of e-mails that will come into our organization. This can be done by using the CREATE module (Figure 4.2).

FIGURE 4.2
Inserting the CREATE module.

One of the most important things that we need to do for a simulation is to create objects that will flow through the simulation that we are creating. In our scenario, the objects flowing through the system are the e-mails that will go through our security devices. In Arena, these objects are known as "entities." To be able to create entities, we need a CREATE module.

To make a CREATE module, all you have to do is drag the icon named create from the left-hand Basic Process bar to your work area. Your work area should look similar to Figure 4.3 below. It still looks a little sparse right now but this is only our first step.

Once you have added the CREATE module, the next step is to start configuring the attributes and properties for that module. To assign value to attributes or properties of the module, double click on the CREATE shape so that a dialog window appears, as shown in Figure 4.4.

In the dialog box, assign any name describing the entity being created. In this case, we labeled the entities as external e-mails. Let us change the entity type to "E-mail" as well. We will also tell the simulation the average rate of e-mail arrival. The arrival of e-mails could be different for each organization. There are different ways of estimating this information (i.e., looking through your logs), but for the purposes of this example, we shall assume that on average an e-mail arrives every second. We can do this by changing the following:

- Type: Random (Expo)
- Value: 1

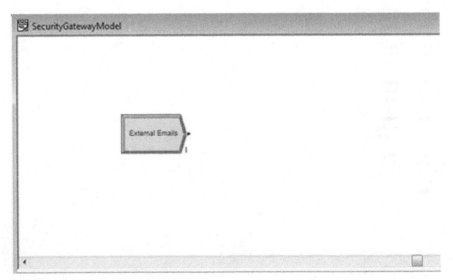

FIGURE 4.3
Using CREATE to create external e-mail entities.

- Units: Seconds
- Entities per Arrival: 1
- Max Arrivals: Infinite
- First Creation: 0.0.

At this point, we have created entities for our simulation. This means that e-mails can now enter our system. But where will it go? Right now, nowhere. We need these e-mails to be processed, so we will need to create a process. This is done by dragging the PROCESS module from the left-hand navigation bar into the workplace as illustrated in Figure 4.5.

Since the e-mails going through the system need to be processed by the AV gateway, we will pattern our process to our gateway. In our simulation, the PROCESS module will represent the AV gateway that will be processing the external e-mails.

Similar to what we did with the CREATE module, we will configure the attributes and properties of the PROCESS module. Open the dialog box for the PROCESS module in the same way you did with the CREATE module by double clicking on it.

First, let us assign a name for the process module. For this example, we will name it "Security Gateway Vendor."

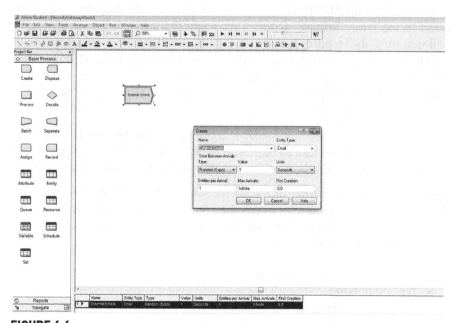

FIGURE 4.4
Updating the properties of the CREATE module.

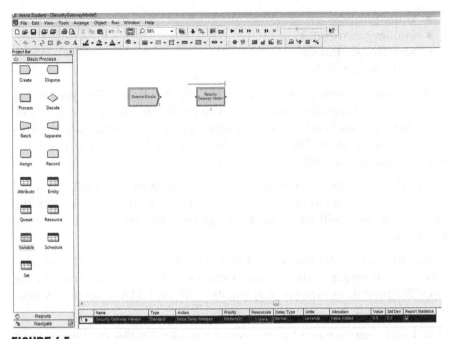

FIGURE 4.5
Adding the PROCESS module.

Next we will set the ACTION for this element. In the action drop down, we will select "Seize, Delay, Release" action. This means that when an e-mail arrives, it will wait until the resource becomes available, it will seize the resource, it will wait for the service interval, and then it will release the resource. This is essentially how an e-mail gateway operates: before a gateway sends an e-mail to the inbox, it will seize, delay (because of processing), and then release either to a user's inbox or a quarantine.

The "Delay" is an important value here in our simulation because it is actually the processing time. Relative to our scenario, this is the length of time the security gateway takes to process an e-mail to find out whether it is malicious or not.

Our next step is to customize our scenario. Since we have the vendor results on the average processing time, let us put the average processing value of Vendor 1 for this example. Your dialog box should look similar to Figure 4.6 and would have the following parameters:

- Name: Security Gateway Vendor
- Type: Standard
- Action: Seize Delay Release
- Priority Medium
- Resources: Resource, Resource 1,1

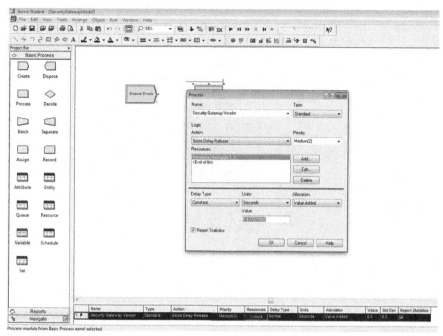

FIGURE 4.6
Updating the properties of the PROCESS module.

- Delay Type: Constant
- Units: Seconds
- Allocation: Value Added
- Report Statistics: Checked
- Value: 0.1777271863.

The next step is to create the resource for our security gateway. Since we are only going to be using one security gateway, we will only create one resource. This setting is important if you are simulating multiple appliances or, in other cases, multiple processors. At this point, for simplicity, we will only create one resource, which can be done by clicking the "Add" button, which is located next to the Resource box. Your Resource dialog box should have the following parameters:

- Type: Resource
- Resource: 1
- Quantity: 1.

As the last step in our PROCESS module, we need to ensure that the CRE-ATE module and the PROCESS module are linked together. In our scenario, this ensures that the e-mails created by the CREATE module goes to the

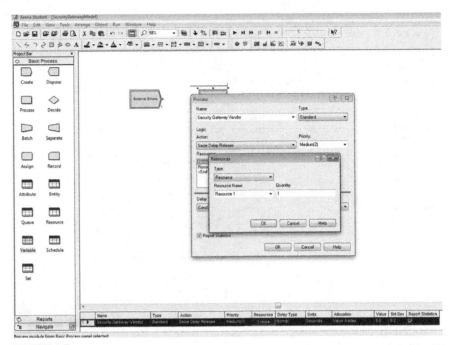

FIGURE 4.7
Updating the resource property of the PROCESS module.

PROCESS module to be processed by our AV gateway (Figure 4.7). Typically, Arena does this automatically; however, if it does not, click the Connect button in the upper toolbar of Arena to link both modules as seen in Figure 4.8.

Finally, after processing, we need somewhere for the e-mails to go. This is where we use the DISPOSE module. Drag a DISPOSE module into your work area and label it as "Mailboxes." Then, connect the PROCESS module with the DISPOSE module. This means that after processing, the e-mails go to the mailboxes.

At this point, you are probably thinking that something is amiss with this scenario. Why would all processed e-mails go directly to the inboxes, right? You are absolutely right that something is amiss. For the sake of keeping our step-by-step tutorial simple, let us work with what we have for now. We will continue to expand on our scenario to make it more realistic. Your final simulation should look similar to the model in Figure 4.9.

Now that we have our simulation model, we are ready to run our first simulation. Before running our simulation, you will need to configure the different settings for the simulation. Since a simulation is technically trying to recreate a

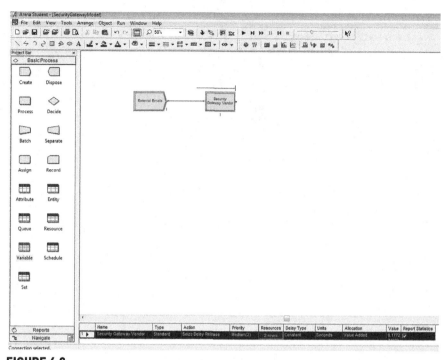

FIGURE 4.8
Connect the CREATE module with the PROCESS module.

real-world scenario, we need to set up how long and how frequently we would like to let the scenario run.

This is fairly easy to do in Arena. Just click on Run (it is a selection on the top bar) and select Run Setup. For this simulation let us run it three times for 7days, 24-hours a day. Since e-mails arrive at a one second interval, the base time unit will need to be changed to seconds. You will see a dialog box similar to Figure 4.10, in which you will add the following parameters:

- Number of Replications: 3
- Initialize Between Replications: Statistics and System Checked
- Warm-up Period: 0.0
- Replication Length: 7
- Hours Per Day: 24
- Base Time Units: Seconds
- Time Units: Hours
- Time Units: Days
- Termination Condition: Leave Blank.

After the Run parameters have been configured, we will add some information on the Project Parameters to describe the project by clicking on the Project

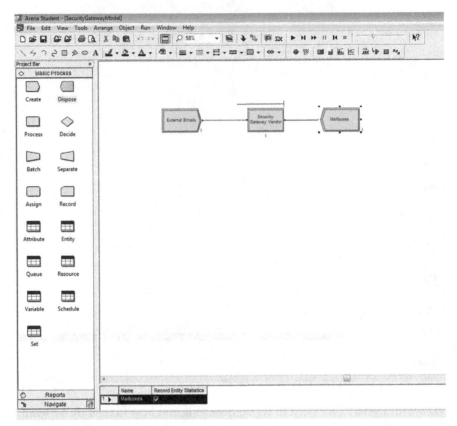

FIGURE 4.9
Connect the CREATE module with the PROCESS module.

Parameter tab (see below figure). We are now ready to run our simulation. You do this by simply clicking Run, then selecting Go.

- Project Title: Security Gateway
- Project Description: Add any description

After clicking Go, the simulation will animate and there will be elements moving. You will see "e-mails" coming from the CREATE module (external e-mails), moving to the PROCESS module (security gateway), and being accepted by the DISPOSE module (inbox) (Figure 4.11).

Congratulations, you have now completed your first simulation! The simulation may take some time to process before we get the results. Unfortunately, even with setting at the highest speed, running three simulations on e-mails over a 7-day period will take some time to process.

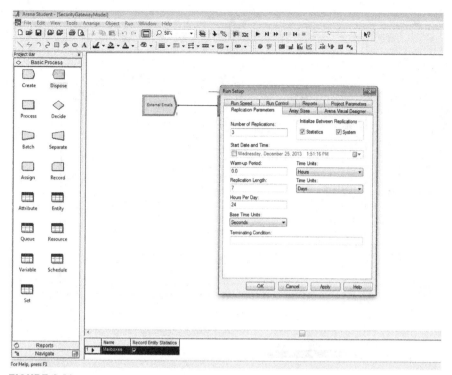

FIGURE 4.10
Run parameters set up.

Fortunately, Arena has a feature, which allows what is called "batch processing." Batch processing bypasses all of the animation, which speeds up processing. To do this, you first need to stop the simulation by clicking on Run, and then End. Next, select Run Control and click on Batch Run (No Animation). By doing this, you will speed up the simulation so that you can generate the results faster (Figure 4.12).

Let us try running the simulation again using these new parameters. You will notice this time that you see no animation and you immediately receive the results.

Your output will be a report, including some interesting values such as minimum averages, maximum averages, minimum values, and maximum values. Basically, these values are the descriptive statistics for your simulation processing times, which we ran three times in 7-day increments (Figure 4.13).

The real value of the simulation is seen once we start comparing the vendors. Let us try doing this next. For each vendor, change the delay value to match each vendor's average processing time. If you gather the results, you should

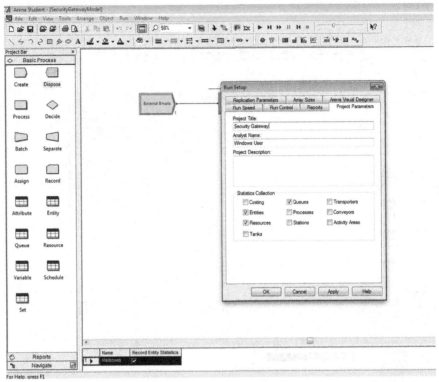

FIGURE 4.11
Project set up.

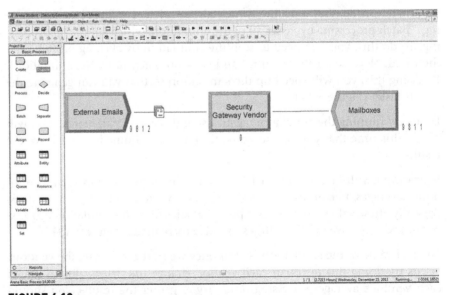

FIGURE 4.12
A running simulation.

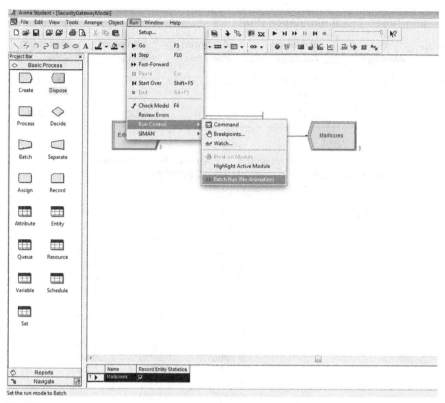

FIGURE 4.13
Doing a batch run.

obtain the results in Table 4.3. Your results should show that Vendor 1's claims are accurate: on average, Vendor 1 shows the best performance.

For now, we will accept that Vendor 1's claim is correct. However, as you know, statistics can sometimes be interpreted to provide misleading information. Let us start by going back and look at the original data that the vendor gave us.

A very interesting point about the original data is that the vendor provided the actual results of their testing. With the results for individual processing times for each of the e-mails, instead of just the average processing time for all of the e-mails, we can use a very simple yet relatively well-known technique called standard deviation (SD).

SD shows the variation or dispersion that exists in relation to the mean (also called average). A low SD indicates the data points tend to be close to the mean (also called expected value); a high SD indicates the data points are spread out over a larger range of values.

Table 4.3 Vendor Processing Time - Initial Simulation Run

	Processing Time	Average	Minimum Average	Maximum Average	Minimum Value	Maximum Value
Vendor 1	0.177271963	0.01911149	0.01897183	0.01919783	0.00	0.9207
Vendor 2	0.669560187	0.6809	0.6760	0.6863	0.00	11.6437
Vendor 3	0.569069159	0.3770	0.3740	0.3740	0.00	8.3927

	Vendor 1	Vendor 2	Vendor 3
Average (sec)	0.177271963	0.669560187	0.569069159
Standard Deviation	=STDEVP(D5:D111)		0.274832835
Test Data (sec)	0.0077	0.0119	0.5994
	0.0018	0.0201	0.5269
	0.0101	3.4405	0.4258
	0.0144	0.0701	0.5109
	0.0134	0.02	0.5619
	0.006	0.0119	0.5017
	0.1103	0.0012	0.4382
	0.0113	0.013	0.4346
	0.0116	0.0161	0.4988
	0.0185	0.0157	0.49
	0.0021	0.2894	0.4843
	0.0088	0.0089	0.4602
	0.0051	0.0056	0.4431
	0.0061	0.0067	1.4135
	0.0106	0.0206	0.4199
	0.0064	0.221	0.4332
	0.01	0.025	0.4162
	0.0128	3.067	0.4386
	0.0113	1.098	0.4342
	0.01	0.0158	0.4309
	0.0058	1.145	0.4146
	0.0023	0.112	0.4392
	0.0126	0.0146	0.4678
	0.0128	0.0098	0.4608
	0.006	0.0201	0.4689
	0.0064	0.0139	0.481
	0.0088	0.0066	0.4449

FIGURE 4.14
Computing SD in a spreadsheet.

Let us start with some simple spreadsheet work. We want to open the file containing the sample data and obtain the SD of the data by using the STDEVP function (=STDEVP). This explanation may be somewhat confusing, so see Figure 4.14. Open the next tab of the sample data containing the computation.

After computing the SD for all of the vendors, we see that Vendor 1 actually has a big SD. This means that the results of the test data vary greatly. For example, it

Table 4.4 Vendor Processing Time - Adding SD

	Average Processing	Standard Deviation	
Vendor 1	0.177271963	1.185744915	
Vendor 2	0.669560187	1.026043254	
Vendor 3	0.569069159	0.274832835	
	Vendor 1	**Vendor 2**	**Vendor 3**
Average (s)	0.177271963	0.669560187	0.569069159
Standard deviation	1.185744915	1.026043254	0.274832835

processes e-mails very fast in some cases, but in other cases, it processes e-mails very slowly. You may be asking yourself, what exactly does this tell us? Obviously, those of you who understand SDs probably already have an inkling of what this means, but we will run a simulation so we can see what our scenario generates (Table 4.4).

Now, we will go back to the simulation to enter our newly computed values. Click on the PROCESS module. However, let us change things up a bit. Instead of using the "Constant" delay type, we will use the "Normal" delay type or what we call a normal distribution. The normal distribution is a function telling you the probability that an observation, in some context, will fall between any two real numbers.

In the PROCESS dialog box, we will maintain the mean value, but we will now add the SD for the vendor. The entries you select should be similar to the below values, which will be put in the dialog box (See Figure 4.15). Next, we will run the simulation.

- Name: Security Gateway Vendor
- Type: Standard
- Action: Seize Delay Release
- Priority: Medium
- Resource: Resource, Resource 1,1
- Delay Type: Normal
- Units: Seconds
- Allocation: Value Added
- Value: 0.177271963
- Std Dev: 1.185744915
- Report Statistics: Checked.

We will run the simulation for all the vendors and collect their results. Remember to make the change to "Normal" for all of the vendors and to add in the SD. Once you have run everything and collected the results, your results should be similar to values in the tables below.

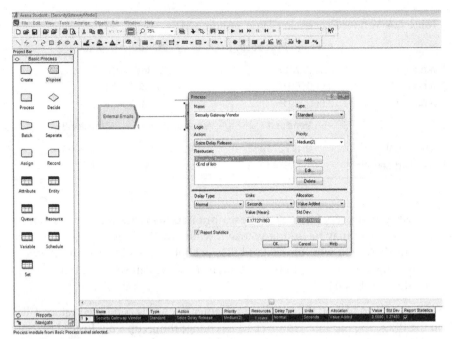

FIGURE 4.15
Updating the PROCESS Dialog's standard deviation.

You should now notice that the results are quite interesting. The values have changed a considerable amount because we used the normal distribution. In fact, Vendor 1 did not perform as well as expected with these results. In this scenario, Vendor 3 actually had better results.

The reason for this is that Vendor 3 had more consistent results. The processing times for Vendor 3 were more stable and, more importantly, less variable. Conversely, Vendor 1 had a lot of variability, which greatly affected the overall processing times. This is why it is important to understand what you are processing and how it will affect your results. Had you just gone with the vendor results, you would not have known this information—this provides you with value-added information, which could affect your choice of a vendor (Table 4.5).

For the final part of our tutorial, we will extend our simulation model to make it more detailed and realistic. In the previous scenario, we assumed that all e-mails were malicious, but in reality we would never do this. For a more realistic scenario, we will incorporate the DECIDE module to create conditional branches.

The DECIDE module can be found in the Basic Process tab, which is located on the left-hand side of our work area. The DECIDE module helps us to create conditions (also known as "if-then" conditions) that are similar to what you would see in a flowchart (Figure 4.16).

Table 4.5 Vendor Processing Time - Additional SD Settings

	Average	Minimum Average	Maximum Average	Minimum Value	Maximum Value
Vendor 1	1.0290	1.0231	1.0342	0.00	25.1238
Vendor 2	3.8393	3.8183	3.8531	0.00	46.5414
Vendor 3	0.4661	0.4650	0.4680	0.00	9.4981
Vendor 1	0.01911149	0.01897183	0.01919783	0.00	0.9207
Vendor 2	0.6809	0.6760	0.6863	0.00	11.6437
Vendor 3	0.3770	0.3740	0.3740	0.00	8.3927

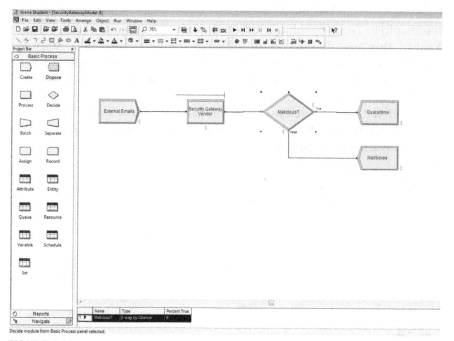

FIGURE 4.16
Adding a DECIDE module in the simulation.

We will now create a scenario with conditional elements. As we already mentioned, not all e-mails will have malicious attachments. Let us say only 5% of all e-mails will have malicious attachments. How did we get 5%? This is entirely dependent on you, but to have a more realistic scenario, you should probably try to check industry benchmarks. For example, Symantec issues a monthly intelligence report similar to the one in this link where you can find benchmarks: http://www.symantec.com/content/en/us/enterprise/other_resources/b-intelligence_report_07-2014.en-us.pdf.

Now, let us go back to our workspace, drag a DECIDE module into the work area, and double click on the module. Once you are at the dialog box, type in a name and change the Type to "2-way chance," which is the default. Since there's a 5% chance of a mail being malicious, you will enter 5% in the Percent True text box. Your entries should be similar to the parameters shown in Figure 4.17.

Finally, we will close of the system by adding a DISPOSE module for both the True and False branches. Note that all simulations must have a DISPOSE module. Let us label the DISPOSE modules as Quarantine for True then Mailbox for false. This will be a little understandable when we start talking about counters.

- Name: Malicious?
- Type: 2-way by Chance
- Percent True (0–100): 5%.

You should be familiar with the RECORD module, which acts like an advance counter. This module used to run different computations and to store the processed results within the module. For this scenario, let us make a simple counter using the RECORD module to track clean and malicious e-mails. If an e-mail is malicious, then we will assume the action to be taken is quarantining the e-mail. If the e-mail is clean, the action to be taken is to send it to the user's inbox. Therefore, we will make two counters: one is a Quarantine counter and the other is a Mailbox counter.

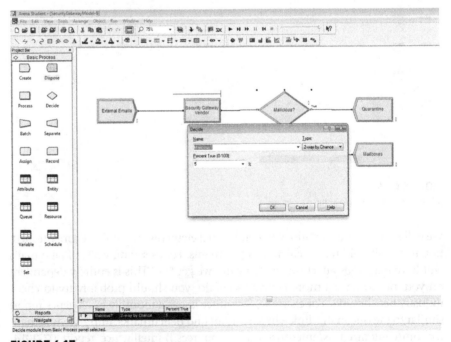

FIGURE 4.17
Updating the properties of a DECIDE module.

We do this by connecting the RECORD modules into the DECIDE module, similar to Figure 4.18. As with all simulations, all paths should have an end point. So, you need to remember to create DISPOSE modules for the two paths: one for the clean e-mails and one for the malicious e-mails.

We will now configure the parameters of our RECORD module. Double click on each of the RECORD modules and set it to "Count" with a value of 1. This means that if the e-mail was malicious, then the RECORD module for the Quarantine RECORD module will be increased by 1. You would do the same for the Mailbox RECORD module. In the context of this scenario, the following applies: if the e-mail is malicious (therefore, YES), then the counter for malicious e-mails will be incremented by 1. If the e-mail is not malicious, then the clean e-mail counter will be incremented by 1 (Figure 4.19).

- Name: Malicious E-mail
- Type: Count
- Value: 1
- Record into Set: Unchecked
- Counter Name: Malicious E-mail.

That is it—our simulation is now complete! We have created a more complex simulation, which utilized the DECISION and RECORD modules. All you have to do now is to run the simulation and wait for the reports to be generated (Figure 4.20).

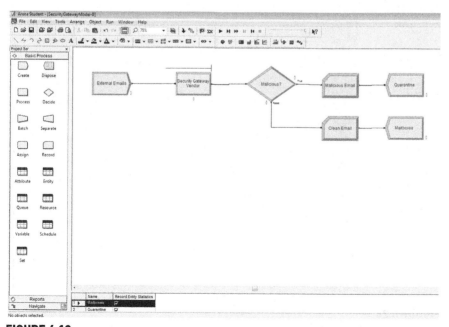

FIGURE 4.18
Creating RECORD and DISPOSE modules.

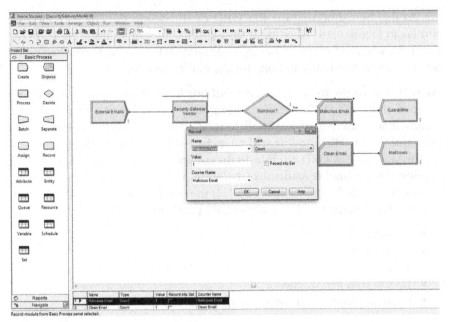

FIGURE 4.19
Updating the properties of the RECORD module.

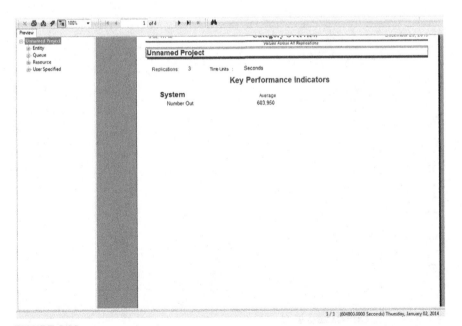

FIGURE 4.20
Viewing the report.

As you can see, our simulation is slowly getting more advanced. However, we are still not finished with it. What about efficacy? The vendor actually provided us with efficacy information and we can use this information to improve our simulation. The question is how do we incorporate this information into our simulation (Figure 4.21)?

In our previous simulation, we assumed that all e-mails that were considered clean were actually clean but in reality, things seldom work this way because malicious e-mail will get through AV checks. This is why the vendor provided us with the ratings of efficacy for each of the products being reviewed. Next, we need to add another conditional element in the simulation so that we may include this process.

We will add another DECIDE module to the second filter for the clean decision, but this time, we will add a condition for every clean e-mail. In this updated scenario, once the decision is made that an e-mail is clean, we place another decision regarding "how sure are we that the e-mail is clean." We will call this our "True Clean" decision box, which is a layer to show the probability that a clean e-mail is actually clean. By adding this decision box, we are able to provide a means to determine "false negatives" or malicious e-mails that were missed by the security gateway. Your updated simulation should look similar to Figure 4.22.

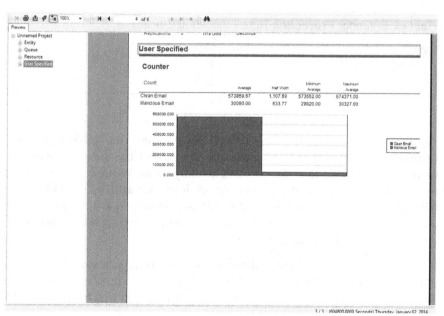

FIGURE 4.21

Additional report information.

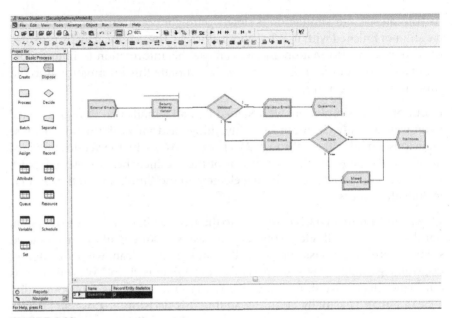

FIGURE 4.22
Removing false negatives through another DECISION module.

Table 4.6 Vendor Processing Time - Including Efficacy	
Vendor 1	99.90%
Vendor 2	99.70%
Vendor 3	98.40%

We will now configure our new DECISION module. Double click the True Clean box and add the efficacy rating into the Percent True box. This will simulate the probability that the e-mail is actually clean. We then add a counter to "how many e-mails that were considered clean were actually malicious." We will use the RECORD module to add a "Missed Malicious E-mail" box. Below are the e-mails that the AV missed, where the vendor's verdict was clean but the e-mails were actually malicious (Table 4.6).

Using our vendor spreadsheet, if the vendor's security gateway has a 99.9% efficacy then we put 99.9% in the Percent True. These values will allow us to compute the probability of an e-mail actually being clean which equates to the efficacy in our simulation. See Figure 4.23.

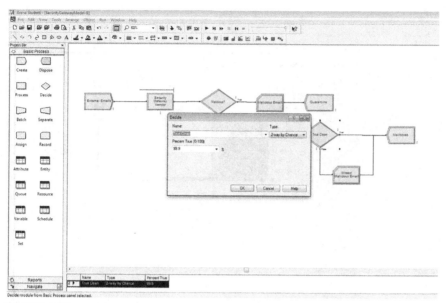

FIGURE 4.23
Adding efficacy into the simulation.

- Name: True Clean
- Type: 2-way by Chance
- Percent True (0–100): 99%.

Finally, let us run our simulation and wait for our report! We will do this for all of our vendors. Remember to make changes to the average processing times, the SD and the efficacy of each simulation.

As we wrap up this chapter, let us go through the completed simulation statistics in Figure 4.24. In summary, here are the observations we obtained from our simulation.

- Vendor 3 is actually pretty good in terms of performance. When we start looking at the efficacy (i.e., 99.9% vs 98%) and considering the amount of e-mails processed in a week, the difference between a 99.9% efficacy and a 98% efficacy rate is a staggering amount. The difference can be as large as 8000 malicious e-mails!
- Even a 99.9% efficacy would result in 568 malicious e-mails, which is still a lot of malicious e-mails. This shows that even when a vendor's AV is used, there is still a big chance that one of your employees could be infected.

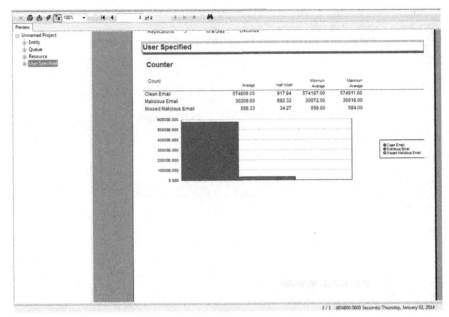

FIGURE 4.24
Viewing the final report.

	Average	Minimum Average	Maximum Average	Minimum Value	Maximum Value	Average Processed in a week	Average Missed Malicious E-mail
Vendor 1	1.0290	1.0231	1.0342	0.00	25.1238	604,918	568.33
Vendor 2	3.8393	3.8183	3.8531	0.00	46.5414	605,514	1704.00
Vendor 3	0.4661	0.4650	0.4680	0.00	9.4981	605,311	9284.00

The following tables provide a summary of the results we collected during the simulation:

Average Processing Times

	Average Processing
Vendor 1	0.177271963
Vendor 2	0.669560187
Vendor 3	0.569069159

Using a Constant Delay Type:

	Average	Minimum Average	Maximum Average	Minimum Value	Maximum Value
Vendor 1	0.01911149	0.01897183	0.01919783	0	0.9207
Vendor 2	0.6809	0.676	0.6863	0	11.6437
Vendor 3	0.377	0.374	0.374	0	8.3927

Using a Normal Distribution (STD):

	Average Processing	Standard Deviation
Vendor 1	0.17727196	1.18574492
Vendor 2	0.66956019	1.02604325
Vendor 3	0.56906916	0.27483284

	Average	Minimum Average	Maximum Average	Minimum Value	Maximum Value
Vendor 1	1.029	1.0231	1.0342	0	25.1238
Vendor 2	3.8393	3.8183	3.8531	0	46.5414
Vendor 3	0.4661	0.465	0.468	0	9.4981

Final Results:

	Average	Minimum Average	Maximum Average	Minimum Value	Maximum Value	Avg. Missed Malicious E-mail
Vendor 1	1.029	1.0231	1.0342	0	25.1238	568.33
Vendor 2	3.8393	3.8183	3.8531	0	46.5414	1704
Vendor 3	0.4661	0.465	0.468	0	9.4981	9284

Data Used in the Simulation:

	Vendor 1	Vendor 2	Vendor 3
Average (s)	0.177271963	0.669560187	0.569069159
Standard deviation	1.185744915	1.026043254	0.274832835
Test data (s)	0.0077	0.0119	0.5994
	0.0018	0.0201	0.5269
	0.0101	3.4405	0.4258
	0.0144	0.0701	0.5109
	0.0134	0.02	0.5619
	0.006	0.0119	0.5017
	0.1103	0.0012	0.4382

Data Used in the Simulation: *Continued*

	Vendor 1	Vendor 2	Vendor 3
	0.0113	0.013	0.4346
	0.0116	0.0161	0.4988
	0.0185	0.0157	0.49
	0.0021	0.2894	0.4843
	0.0088	0.0089	0.4602
	0.0051	0.0056	0.4431
	0.0061	0.0067	1.4135
	0.0106	0.0206	0.4199
	0.0064	0.221	0.4332
	0.01	0.025	0.4162
	0.0128	3.067	0.4386
	0.0113	1.098	0.4342
	0.01	0.0158	0.4309
	0.0058	1.145	0.4146
	0.0023	0.112	0.4392
	0.0126	0.0146	0.4678
	0.0128	0.0098	0.4608
	0.006	0.0201	0.4689
	0.0064	0.0139	0.481
	0.0088	0.0066	0.4449
	0.011	1.945	0.4312
	0.0142	0.8112	0.453
	0.0058	0.855	1.2839
	0.0062	0.874	0.445
	0.0063	1.589	0.4275
	0.014	0.0203	0.4517
	0.0946	0.89	1.092
	0.0011	0.0112	0.5119
	0.0073	2.547	0.5966
	0.0089	3.4003	1.2248
	0.0111	2.3314	0.4345
	0.0081	0.0158	0.5527
	0.0114	0.0144	0.4991
	0.0096	0.0204	0.4213
	0.6305	0.0061	1.3264
	0.0113	0.0105	0.4312
	0.0059	2.578	0.4246
	0.0102	0.95	0.4422
	0.065	0.721	1.4509
	0.0063	3.3614	0.478
	0.0189	0.3078	0.4121
	0.9503	3.3444	1.1532

Data Used in the Simulation: *Continued*

	Vendor 1	Vendor 2	Vendor 3
	0.0236	0.0103	0.4589
	0.0094	0.00254	0.4124
	0.0076	1.067	0.5074
	0.0057	0.905	0.4509
	1.0007	3.4747	0.4639
	0.0061	0.0205	0.4729
	0.0113	0.013	0.4343
	0.0094	0.0018	0.4359
	0.0061	0.0101	0.4761
	0.0088	1.345	0.4594
	0.0054	0.0936	0.6192
	0.9407	3.7085	1.1916
	12.2007	3.4655	0.5122
	0.0035	1.523	0.4097
	0.0028	0.0202	0.4422
	0.0042	0.0147	0.4585
	0.083	0.9678	1.282
	0.0009	0.0059	1.4524
	0.0078	0.0211	0.5503
	0.0357	0.0496	0.7331
	0.0068	0.016	0.4823
	0.0107	0.0177	0.4378
	0.0128	1.8678	0.4388
	0.0113	0.013	0.4349
	0.9457	0.812	0.9953
	0.0109	0.0071	0.4457
	0.0181	1.78	0.4099
	0.0099	0.0102	0.4278
	0.0066	0.832	0.4231
	0.0111	0.0127	0.4346
	0.0108	0.0144	0.4988
	0.0159	0.0026	1.4738
	0.0155	0.0772	0.4918
	0.0113	0.0136	0.4157
	0.0057	0.0101	0.4327
	0.0064	0.0125	0.5496
	0.0126	0.0146	0.4308
	0.0171	0.042	0.4525
	0.0038	0.1454	0.6053
	0.0059	1.89	0.4243
	0.0043	0.0407	0.7431
	0.0066	0.8901	0.4764

Continued...

Data Used in the Simulation: *Continued*

	Vendor 1	Vendor 2	Vendor 3
	0.0069	0.8542	0.4635
	0.01	0.0059	0.522
	0.0064	1.956	0.4802
	0.0119	1.993	0.4333
	0.0113	1.432	0.4343
	0.0111	0.0127	0.4347
	0.0064	0.0125	0.5521
	0.065	0.711	1.2924
	0.0912	0.0056	0.5121
	0.0059	0.0107	0.4661
	0.0125	0.0124	0.4177
	0.0113	0.013	0.4157
	0.8998	1.9081	0.4626
	0.0059	0.0102	0.4304
	0.0184	1.145	0.4216
	0.0099	0.0144	0.5201

In this chapter, we demonstrated how it is possible to simulate performance when it is difficult to test a system or otherwise obtain results. In our security scenario, we simulated an AV gateway for three vendors; however, there are a lot of other interesting uses for simulations. Another possible use of simulations in security could be recreating virus propagation within a network to see how fast it will affect your enterprise. You could also use simulations to see the effects of patching, of re-imaging machines and of AV updates. On a larger scale, simulations could be used to demonstrate cyber attacks against your organization. You can create a simulation representing your whole network, including firewalls, a intrusion prevention system and network segments, to see how attacks would or would not be detected, among other things. In conclusion, simulations in security are particularly useful in evaluating the effect of security controls or mechanisms in your enterprise that would, otherwise, be difficult to recreate.

Access Analytics

INTRODUCTION

There are so many ways that malicious users can access IT systems right now. In fact, the very technologies affording us the convenience to remotely access our IT systems are the ones that are being manipulated by malicious users. In today's IT environment, physical access is no longer a hindrance to gaining access to internal resources and data.

Remote access technologies such as virtual private network (VPN) are commonly used in business environments. While these technologies provide increased efficiency in terms of productivity, they also introduce another level of risk into an organization. There have been many incidents lately stemming from remote access intrusions. In fact, several studies indicate that the majority of data breaches were linked to third-party components of IT system administration.

It is important to have a security program where we can quickly identify misuse of system access. In so doing, we are able to limit any damage that could be done through an unauthorized access. But how can you, as a security professional, track anomalous behavior and detect attacks? We need to have efficient ways of monitoring remote access data.

Unfortunately, many current products for third-party remote access do not offer granular security settings and comprehensive audit trails. If they do, they do not have advanced misuse or anomaly detection capabilities that will help security professionals identify potential unauthorized access scenarios.

In this chapter, we would like to provide some techniques and tools that could help you in these types of scenarios. Some of the things we will explore include knowledge engineering, by means of programming detection strategies. If you do not know how to program, do not worry. We will provide simple techniques and step-by-step walk-through instruction to get you going.

TECHNOLOGY PRIMER

First off, we will provide a brief background of the technologies involved in our scenario. As you can tell by the introduction, we will be focusing on detecting unauthorized access in remote access technologies.

You may already be familiar with some of the technologies that we will be using in our scenario: they include remote access, VPN, and python. Our main data set in our scenario is VPN logs. We will use Python to create a program that will process the VPN logs. Our goal is to use a variety of techniques to identify anomalies in our data set.

First off, let us talk about our data and the technology that is involved in it.

Remote Access and VPN
What is VPN?
Basically, VPN is a generic term to describe a combination of technologies allowing one to create a secure tunnel through an unsecured or untrusted network, such as public networks like the Internet. This technology is used in lieu of a dedicated connection, commonly referred to as a dedicated line, from which the technology derives its "virtual" name. By using this technology, traffic appears to be running through a "private" network.

How does VPN work?
Data in VPN are transmitted via tunneling. Packets are encapsulated or wrapped in another packet with a new header that provides routing information. The route that these packets travel through is what is considered as the tunnel. There are also different tunneling protocols, but since this is not within the scope of this book, we will not be covering these protocols. Another thing to note about VPNs is that the data are encrypted. Basically, data going through the tunnel, which is passed through a public network, are unreadable without proper decryption keys. This ensures that data confidentiality and integrity is maintained.

What are the Dangers of VPN?

Using VPN in general is considered good practice for remote access. This makes packets going through a public network such as the Internet unreadable without proper decryption keys. It also ensures data are not disclosed or changed during transmission. However, by default, VPN generally does not provide or enforce strong user authentication. Current VPN technologies support add-on two-factor authentication mechanisms, such as tokens and various other mechanisms, which were mentioned earlier. However, by default, it is simply a username and password for gaining access to the internal network. This can present a significant risk because there could be scenarios whereby an attacker gains access to these credentials and subsequently to your internal resources. Here are a few examples:

- A user can misplace their username and password.
- A user can purposely share their username and password.
- A user can fall victim to a spear phishing attack.
- A user might be using a compromised machine with malware harvesting credentials.

In any of the above scenarios, once an attacker obtains the user's credentials, assuming there is no two-factor authentication, the attacker would be able to gain access to all internal resources to which the user currently has access via the user's remote profiles and access rights. Thus, determining the access rights is a major factor in determining the potential extent of the compromise.

Monitoring VPN

As this chapter is about detecting potential unauthorized remote access, it is important to provide you with a brief background on logging VPN access. Most VPN solutions have, in one form or another, logging capabilities. Although much of the logging capability is dependent on the vendor, at the very least, your VPN logs should contain the following information:

- user ID of the individual,
- date and time of access,
- what resources were accessed, and
- the external IP from which the access was made.

There are many VPN solutions, so it would be impossible to outline all the necessary instructions to obtain your organization's VPN log data, but your network administrator should be able to provide log data to you. For the purposes of this chapter, we will be providing you with a sample data set that contains the aforementioned data.

In general, log data are fairly easy to obtain. However, monitoring the logs to ensure that the people who are logging on are actually employees of your organization is another matter. Let us say your organization has 5000 employees and one-quarter of them are given VPN access. There are still over 1000 connections that you will have to review. Obviously, you will not be able to ask each and every employee if they made the connection, right? We certainly do not lack the data; however, we are limited by our analysis capabilities. This lack of analysis is what we will be focusing on in this chapter.

Python and Scripting

In most cases, we are stuck with whatever data that we have. If your VPN software provides robust detection and analytics capability helping you to identify potentially anomalous access cases, then your organization is off to a great start. Oftentimes, you just have a spreadsheet of VPN access, similar to what we will be providing to you in this chapter. Therefore, we will show you how to build this capability, with a little bit of programming, so that you may conduct your own analysis.

Typically, programming is not what 99% of security professionals do for a living. Unless you work directly in recreating vulnerabilities or exploits in software, it is a skill that most of us know about but rarely use. We believe that learning to program is a valuable and useful skill for security professionals. You do not need to know how to program complex software, but programming can help you to automate efforts that would otherwise take a lot of time. For example, let us say we wanted to review all of our VPN logs. This could be a significant task, so providing some degree of automation, particularly if the logic is repetitive, would really help you. In this regard, knowing how to program or use a "scripting language" would greatly benefit you in making the process more efficient.

What is a Scripting Language?

There is still some ambiguity on what can be considered a scripting language. In principle, any programming language can be used as a scripting language. A scripting language is designed as an extension language for specific environments. Typically, a scripting language is a programming language used for task automation, as opposed to tasks executed one-by-one by a human operator. For example, these could be tasks a system administrator can be doing in an operating system. For our purpose, you can think of a scripting language as a general-purpose language.

Scripting languages are often used to connect system components, and are sometimes called "glue languages." One good example is Perl, which has been used a lot for this purpose. Scripting languages are also used as a "wrapper" program for various executables. Additionally, scripting languages are intended to be simple to pick up and easy to write. A good example of a scripting language that is fairly easy to pick up is Python. So, this is the language that we are going to use in our scenario.

Python

Python is relatively easy to learn while being a powerful programming language. The syntax allows programmers to create programs in fewer lines than it would be possible in other languages. It also features a fairly large, comprehensive library and third-party tools. It has interpreters for multiple operating systems, so if you are using a Windows-, Mac-, or Linux-based machine, you should be able to access and use Python. Finally, Python is free, and since it is open source, it may be freely distributed.

Python is an interpreted language, meaning you do not have to compile it, unlike more traditional languages like C or C++. Python is geared for rapid development, saving you considerable time in program development. As such, it is perfect for simple automation tasks, such as those we have planned for in our scenario for this chapter. Aside from this, the interpreter can be used interactively, providing an interface for easy experimentation.

Resources

As this book is not a Python tutorial book, we will point you to really good resources that will help you to start using Python. The following are lists of recommended resources:

Codecademy

A great resource that we highly recommend to start with is the Python track of Codecademy:

- http://www.codecademy.com/en/tracks/python

Codecademy is an online interactive Web site for learning programming languages. One of the key resources is Codecademy's online tool, which provides a sandbox in your browser, where you can actually test your code. The site also has a forum for coding enthusiasts and beginners, which is helpful when you encounter problems.

Python.org

Python.org is the official Web site for Python. Python is a very well-documented language—it is apparent in the amount of documentation available on the site. The full documentation for Python 3.4 (the stable version during the time of this writing) is available on the following link:

- https://docs.python.org/3.4/

As you will see, the documentation is comprehensive. When you become more experienced with Python, this will be a great source of information. However, before you go too deep, you should go to this link for a basic tutorial to first get your feet wet:

- https://docs.python.org/3.4/tutorial/index.html

Learning Python the Hard Way

Contrary to the title, this is actually a really good resource in learning Python. It is a beginners programming course that includes videos and a downloadable book. Following is the main Web site:

- http://learnpythonthehardway.org

But if you do not want to pay for the videos and the downloadable book, the content is also available on an online version here:

- http://learnpythonthehardway.org/book/

The course consists of about 52 exercises. Depending on your skill level and the amount of time you want to invest in learning the language, the author claims it can take as little as one week, and as long as six months. Nonetheless, it is a very good resource and should be something that you should consider reviewing.

Things to Learn

At the very least, you should consider learning the following Python topics: Python syntax, strings, conditionals, control flow, functions, lists, and loops.

If this is your first time with a scripting language, do not worry. You do not have to be an expert in Python to be able to continue with this chapter. As we go through the scenario, we will be explaining what each piece of the sample code is doing. But before that, let us go into more detail on our scenario and the techniques we will actually use to solve the problem.

SCENARIO, ANALYSIS, AND TECHNIQUES

Let us discuss the overall scenario we will be using. We will break this down based on the questions we need to answer:

- What is the problem?
- What are the data that we will be using and how do we collect them?
- How will we analyze the data? What techniques are we using?
- How will we be able to practically apply the analysis technique to the data?
- How to deliver the results?

Problem

In our scenario, we want to show how to identify potentially unauthorized remote accesses to an organization.

Data Collection

The data we will be using for our scenario are the VPN access logs. At a minimum, the data will contain the following information:

- User ID
- Date and time of access
- Internal resource accessed (internal IP)
- Source IP (external IP)

We will assume that the below-listed data were provided to us as a spreadsheet, as this is the most common way for exporting data. For now, you can leverage the data set provided as part of this book. Here is a sample extract from that data set (Figure 5.1):

Data Analysis

Before we go into identifying potentially anomalous VPN logins, let us think about a simpler scenario. If you were going through your credit card transaction statements and saw the below-listed events, what would you have concluded?

- Your credit card was used at the same time at two different locations;
- Your credit card was used in Russia (and you have never been there);
- Your credit card was used in two different physical locations in the same hour when it is physically impossible to get there in an hour; and
- Your credit card was used a hundred different times in the course of the week.

These are indicators that your credit card may have been compromised. While this is a simplistic example, we will be extending this type of analysis in our scenario by looking for anomalous behavior indicating a compromise.

So now, let us review our VPN access logs. Let us assume that you only had to review your access. How would you review the VPN access logs manually? What would you look for? It would be fairly straightforward, right? Let us use the same fact pattern we used for the credit card transactions.

- Your user ID logged in concurrently from two different IP addresses;
- Your user ID logged in from Russia (and you have never been there);
- Your user ID was used twice in an hour from your office and your home when it is physically impossible to get there in an hour; and
- Your user ID logged in from a hundred different IP addresses in the course of the week.

It makes sense, right? This is just plain logic and common sense, assuming we are only looking for the narrow fact patterns listed above. If you think about it, there could be other scenarios in which you could look for similar anomalous

Id	EventType Id	EventType Ev	EventType O	Device Id	Device Zone	EventSource	EventSource	EventDestini	EventDestini	Protocol	ReceiveTime	DeviceTime	RawMessage	Transmitted	SessionDurat Session	SessionSourc	SessionSourc	SessionDesti
6748267218	2	279656	2	0	1044460	988	default_local	0.0.0.0	0.0.0.0	0	0	-1 Apr 3, 2013	1 Never	<165>c.5	0	0/#######.#	0	0.0.0.0	0.0.0.0
6748163045	279656	1720274		0	1044460	988	default_local	0.0.0.0	0.0.0.0	0	0	0 Apr 3, 2013	1 Never	<165>c.5	0	0/#######.#	0	0.0.0.0	0.0.0.0
6748129176	279656	1720274		0	1044460	988	default_local	0.0.0.0	0.0.0.0	0	0	0 Apr 3, 2013	1 Never	<165>c.5	0	0/#######.#	0	0.0.0.0	0.0.0.0
6748110303	279656	1720274		0	1044460	988	default_local	0.0.0.0	0.0.0.0	0	0	0 Apr 3, 2013	1 Never	<165>c.5	0	0/#######.#	0	0.0.0.0	0.0.0.0
6748036303	2	2		0	1044460	988	default_local	0.0.0.0	0.0.0.0	0	0	-1 Apr 3, 2013	1 Never	<164>c.5	0	0/#######.#	0	0.0.0.0	0.0.0.0
6747985571	2	2		0	1044460	988	default_local	0.0.0.0	0.0.0.0	0	0	-1 Apr 3, 2013	1 Never	<164>c.5	0	0/#######.#	0	0.0.0.0	0.0.0.0
6747893397	2	2		0	1044460	988	default_local	0.0.0.0	0.0.0.0	0	0	-1 Apr 3, 2013	1 Never	<165>c.5	0	0/#######.#	0	0.0.0.0	0.0.0.0
6747857694	279656	1720274		0	1044460	988	default_local	0.0.0.0	0.0.0.0	0	0	0 Apr 3, 2013	1 Never	<164>c.5	0	0/#######.#	0	0.0.0.0	0.0.0.0
6747840082	2	2		0	1044460	988	default_local	0.0.0.0	0.0.0.0	0	0	-1 Apr 3, 2013	1 Never	<164>c.5	0	0/#######.#	0	0.0.0.0	0.0.0.0
6747834011	279656	1720274		0	1044460	988	default_local	0.0.0.0	0.0.0.0	0	0	0 Apr 3, 2013	1 Never	<165>c.5	0	0/#######.#	0	0.0.0.0	0.0.0.0
6747833672	2	2		0	1044460	988	default_local	0.0.0.0	0.0.0.0	0	0	-1 Apr 3, 2013	1 Never	<164>c.5	0	0/#######.#	0	0.0.0.0	0.0.0.0
6747722297	2	2		0	1044460	988	default_local	0.0.0.0	0.0.0.0	0	0	-1 Apr 3, 2013	1 Never	<164>c.5	0	0/#######.#	0	0.0.0.0	0.0.0.0
6747705217	2	2		0	1044460	988	default_local	0.0.0.0	0.0.0.0	0	0	-1 Apr 3, 2013	1 Never	<164>c.5	0	0/#######.#	0	0.0.0.0	0.0.0.0
6747686497	2	2		0	1044460	988	default_local	0.0.0.0	0.0.0.0	0	0	0 Apr 3, 2013	1 Never	<164>c.5	0	0/#######.#	0	0.0.0.0	0.0.0.0
6747685723	279656	1720274		0	1044460	988	default_local	0.0.0.0	0.0.0.0	0	0	0 Apr 3, 2013	1 Never	<165>c.5	0	0/#######.#	0	0.0.0.0	0.0.0.0
6747489411	279656	1720274		0	1044460	988	default_local	0.0.0.0	0.0.0.0	0	0	0 Apr 3, 2013	1 Never	<165>c.5	0	0/#######.#	0	0.0.0.0	0.0.0.0
6747477077	279656	1720274		0	1044460	988	default_local	0.0.0.0	0.0.0.0	0	0	0 Apr 3, 2013	1 Never	<165>c.5	0	0/#######.#	0	0.0.0.0	0.0.0.0
6747295147	2	2		0	1044460	988	default_local	0.0.0.0	0.0.0.0	0	0	-1 Apr 3, 2013	1 Never	<164>c.5	0	0/#######.#	0	0.0.0.0	0.0.0.0
6747220092	2	2		0	1044460	988	default_local	0.0.0.0	0.0.0.0	0	0	-1 Apr 3, 2013	1 Never	<164>c.5	0	0/#######.#	0	0.0.0.0	0.0.0.0
6747101375	2	2		0	1044460	988	default_local	0.0.0.0	0.0.0.0	0	0	-1 Apr 3, 2013	1 Never	<164>c.5	0	0/#######.#	0	0.0.0.0	0.0.0.0
6747076503	279656	1720274		0	1044460	988	default_local	0.0.0.0	0.0.0.0	0	0	0 Apr 3, 2013	1 Never	<165>c.5	0	0/#######.#	0	0.0.0.0	0.0.0.0
6747063995	279656	1720274		0	1044460	988	default_local	0.0.0.0	0.0.0.0	0	0	0 Apr 3, 2013	1 Never	<165>c.5	0	0/#######.#	0	0.0.0.0	0.0.0.0
6746836462	279656	1720274		0	1044460	988	default_local	0.0.0.0	0.0.0.0	0	0	0 Apr 3, 2013	1 Never	<165>c.5	0	0/#######.#	0	0.0.0.0	0.0.0.0
6746394180	279656	1720274		0	1044460	988	default_local	0.0.0.0	0.0.0.0	0	0	0 Apr 3, 2013	1 Never	<165>c.5	0	0/#######.#	0	0.0.0.0	0.0.0.0
6746442907	2	2		0	1044460	988	default_local	0.0.0.0	0.0.0.0	0	0	-1 Apr 3, 2013	1 Never	<164>c.5	0	0/#######.#	0	0.0.0.0	0.0.0.0
6746412541	2	2		0	1044460	988	default_local	0.0.0.0	0.0.0.0	0	0	-1 Apr 3, 2013	1 Never	<164>c.5	0	0/#######.#	0	0.0.0.0	0.0.0.0
6746222405	279656	1720274		0	1044460	988	default_local	0.0.0.0	0.0.0.0	0	0	0 Apr 3, 2013	1 Never	<164>c.5	0	0/#######.#	0	0.0.0.0	0.0.0.0
6746191465	279656	1720274		0	1044460	988	default_local	0.0.0.0	0.0.0.0	0	0	-1 Apr 3, 2013	1 Never	<164>c.5	0	0/#######.#	0	0.0.0.0	0.0.0.0
6746165611	279656	1720274		0	1044460	988	default_local	0.0.0.0	0.0.0.0	0	0	0 Apr 3, 2013	1 Never	<165>c.5	0	0/#######.#	0	0.0.0.0	0.0.0.0
6746080566	279656	1720274		0	1044460	988	default_local	0.0.0.0	0.0.0.0	0	0	0 Apr 3, 2013	1 Never	<165>c.5	0	0/#######.#	0	0.0.0.0	0.0.0.0

FIGURE 5.1

Sample data set: VPN logs.

behavior. For example, listed below are sample questions that could lead us to finding anomalous user connections:

- How much time does a user's session usually take?
- What time does a given user usually log in?
- At what time does a given user's connection usually originate?
- At what time does a given source IP address usually originate?
- At what time do all connections usually originate from?
- At what time do connections from a certain city (based on the IP address) usually originate?
- What is the relationship between log-in time and access time of an internal system?
- What time does a given user usually log off?
- What time does a source IP address usually log off?
- What time does a user's country usually log off?
- What time does a user's city usually log off?
- What time does an internally accessed system have in common with the log-off time from the VPN?
- From what source IP address does a given user originate?
- From what country does a given user originate?
- From what city does a given user originate?
- What internal system does a given username usually access?
- What is the IP address with which a country is usually associated?
- What is the IP address with which a city is usually associated?
- What users connected to an internal system?
- With what country is a given city associated?
- Which internal systems are accessed from which country?
- Which internal systems are accessed from certain cities?

As you can see, we have raised multiple questions that could indicate a potentially suspicious connection. But for now, let us focus on one potentially critical factor: distance of connection. Obviously, even if a user was working remotely, it would be suspicious if a user logs in from multiple locations when it is physically impossible to be there. Of course, there could be exceptions. For example, a user could log in from one machine at a particular location, log off that machine, and then log in from different machine at a different location; however, this is suspicious, in itself.

So, first we need to ask ourselves what would be a good way to determine if the distance between locations is significant. For this, we can use haversine distances.

Haversine Distances

Haversine distance is a formula for finding the great-circle distance between a pair of latitude–longitude coordinates. Basically, it is a calculation of geographic distance (latitude and longitude), which incorporates the concept of measuring spherical distance (as the Earth is nonperfect sphere). This equation is important in navigation, but can be applied in other applications. For example, it can be used to determine accessibility of health-care facilities within a certain geographical area. The haversine distance technique can also be used in crime analysis applications, such as finding incidents taking place within a particular distance.

We will not go through the math involved in calculating a haversine distance, but we will cover how we can apply this to our problem. Simply put, the greater the haversine distance, the greater the distance between the sources of the remote logins. And, the greater the distance between the remote logins of one particular user in a given time span, the greater are the chances that this was a potentially anomalous user access.

Data Processing

So now, we have the data (the VPN logs) and we have our analysis technique (haversine distances). But how do we put these together? This is when our scripting or "glue" language comes into play. In order to process the data, we will have to create a script that will do the following things:

- Import the data: First, we will need to be able to import the VPN logs so that our program can process it. For example, if the data are in the form of a spreadsheet, then we will need to be able load the data from the spreadsheet into memory so that we can preprocess the data and then apply our analysis technique.
- Preprocess the data: "Preprocessing" is making the data better structured, so it can be used by our analysis technique. For example, our VPN logs would only have source IPs. In order to actually get the haversine distance, we will need to be able to get the latitude and longitude values. Aside from that, we will need to do some error checking and validation to make sure the data we are entering for analysis are valid. As they say, "garbage in, garbage out."
- Apply the analysis technique: Once we have all the necessary data, we will then use our analysis technique, which in this case is the haversine distance.
- Generating the results: Finally, once we get the haversine distance, we will need to determine a threshold for what is unusual for a certain amount of time. Obviously, we will look for a greater haversine distance in a shorter log-in frequency span as being more suspicious.

We have covered the basic steps we will be following in developing our Python program. In the next section, we start diving into the innards of our Python program. If you have some programming knowledge and can follow a program's flow (i.e., loops and conditions), you should be able to follow the case study even without any Python knowledge. If you do not have the programming knowledge, feel free to go through the primer resources provided in the previous section.

CASE STUDY

Importing What You Need

```
import argparse
import re
import csv
import math
from datetime import datetime
```

Now let us go over the code. First off, you will see several import statements. In most programming languages, a programmer is not expected to do everything from scratch. For example, if someone has already built scripts to handle processing of date and time, typically one does not have to write them from scratch. Oftentimes, there are "modules" a programmer can "import," so they can reuse the scripts and incorporate them into other programs or scripts. This is basically what is happening with the programming code outlined above.

Python code gains access to the functionality provided by one module through the process of importing the module. The import statement, as seen, here is the most common way of invoking the import functionality.

Let us go through each of the modules that we are importing:

- The **argparse module** is used to create command-line interfaces for your script like:

```
python yourporgramname.py arguments
```

This module automatically defines what arguments it requires, generates help and usage messages, and issues errors when a user gives the program invalid arguments. We will use this module to accept arguments from our command line, such as the name of the VPN log file that we are going to process.

- The **re module** provides regular expression support to Python programs. A regular expression specifies a set of strings that matches it. Basically the functions in this module allow you to check if there are particular string matches that correspond to the given regular expression. If you have limited exposure to regular expressions, there is a good amount of reference material available from the Web. Since our VPN logs are mostly unstructured text, we will be using this module to parse the events in our VPN logs to produce a more structured data set.
- The **csv module** provides support and various functionalities for reading, writing, and manipulating CSV or "comma separated values." The CSV format is probably the most common import and export format for spreadsheets and databases. It should be noted though that there is no

standard CSV format, so it can vary from application to application. There are CSV files where delimiters are not even commas—they can be spaces, tabs, semicolons (;), carets (^), or pipes (|). The overall format is similar enough for this module to read and write tabular data. We will be using this module in our scenario to process VPN logs formatted using CSV and we will produce the results in the same format, as well.

- The **math module** provides access to the mathematical functions defined by the C standard. We need the math module for the computations we will be doing in the script, particularly when we use the haversine distance formula.

- The **datetime module** supplies classes for manipulating dates and times, in both simple and complex ways. While date and time arithmetic is supported, the focus of this implementation is on efficient attribute extraction for output formatting and manipulation. For related functionalities, see the time and calendar modules.

```
# requires maxmind geoip database and library
# http://dev.maxmind.com/geoip/legacy/install/city/
import GeoIP
```

We will also be using a third-party module called GeoIP for our program. This is the MaxMind's GeoIP module, which will enable our program to identify the geographic information from an IP address. Most importantly, we are concerned with the latitude and longitude for our haversine distance computation, but it also allows us to identify the location, organization, and connection speed. MaxMind's GeoIP module is one of the more popular geolocation databases. More information can be seen in this link:

- http://dev.maxmind.com/geoip/geoip2/geolite2/

For our scenario, we will be using the GeoLite 2 database, which is a free geolocation database also from MaxMind. It is comparable, but it is less accurate than the company's premier product, which is the GeoIP2 database.

To get started with MaxMind GeoIP, go through this link and install it into your system:

- http://dev.maxmind.com/geoip/legacy/install/city/

The link above provides a brief outline of the steps needed to install GeoIP City on Linux or Unix systems. The installation on Windows is similar: You will just need to use WinZip or a similar ZIP program. The outline provides the following steps:

- Download database
- Install database
- Query database

Program Flow

```python
def main():
""" Main program function """
args = parse_args()

# read report
header, rows = read_csv(args.report)

# normalize event data
events = normalize(header, rows)

# perform analytics
events = analyze(events)

# write output
write_csv(args.out, events)

if __name__ == '__main__':
main()
```

The main function provides the flow of the actual program. The diagram below illustrates how the program will work (Figure 5.2).

The flow is fairly straightforward, since it is a very simple program. Here is an additional description of the overall program flow.

- The program will read and parse the command-line argument. This is how the program knows which VPN log it will need to process.
- Once the name of the file has been passed through the argument, the program will then read the file.
- While reading the file, the program will start normalizing the contents of the VPN logs. This means that the data are converted to the format that will be more conducive for processing.
- Once the data are normalized, the program will then run the analysis which in this case consists of GeoIP processing, which includes identifying the latitude and longitude, as well as the computation for the haversine distance.
- Finally, we will generate the report that will show the accounts that have the highest haversine distance.

FIGURE 5.2
The remote access Python analytics program flow.

In the subsequent sections, we will go through a more detailed review of each process and code snippets one-by-one.

Parse the Arguments

Let us go through the code that reads and parses the command-line argument. We parse the arguments using the "call" from the main.

```
args = parse_args()
```

The function we are calling is called **parse_args()**:

```
def parse_args():
  # parse commandline options
  parser = argparse.ArgumentParser()
  parser.add_argument('report',
type=argparse.FileType('rb'),
      help='csv report to parse')
  parser.add_argument('-o', '--out', default='out.csv',
      type=argparse.FileType('w'),
      help='csv report output file')
  return parser.parse_args()
```

Basically, this code snippet allows the program to be able to take a command-line argument. In our case, there are two arguments that we would like to be able to pass:

- The name of the VPN log file that we would like to process
- The name of the output file where the results will be written

The important part here, in the code, is the **parser.add.argument** method. You will notice that we have two statements corresponding to the two arguments we need to take.

Overall, this would allow us to issue a command in the following manner:

```
python analyze.py vpn.csv -o out.csv
```

You will also see that the "-o" is not required, because it will default to "out.csv," as you will see in the second "add.argument" statement in the program.

Read the VPN Logs

Let us go through the code that reads the file that is containing the VPN logs. This is done through the following statements in main:

```
# read report
  header, rows = read_csv(args.report)
The function that is called read_csv():
```

```
def read_csv(file):
  """ Reads a CSV file and returns the header and rows """
  with file:
    reader = csv.reader(file)
    header = reader.next()
    rows = list(reader)
  return header, rows
```

This snippet of code allows the program to read the CSV file. Here are the various processes the code implements:

- A CSV object called "reader" is created. This uses the CSV module that was imported previously. The CSV module provides methods to manipulate tabular data.
- The reader object iterates over the lines in the given CSV file. Each row read from the CSV file is returned as a list of strings.
- Since the first row of our data file contains a header (the title of the rows), the program iterates to the first line and gets the header information. This is stored in the "header" variable.
- The contents of the file or the logs itself are then loaded into the "rows" variable.

At the end of all this, we loaded the entire content of the VPN log file into memory and returned it to the program for further processing.

Normalize the Event Data from the VPN logs

After we have loaded all the data into memory, the next step is to normalize the event data. This is done by calling the following code from main:

```
# normalize event data
events = normalize(header, rows)
```

The function to normalize data is called **normalize()**:

```
def normalize(header, rows):
  """ Normalizes the data """
  events = []
  for row in rows:
    timestamp = row[header.index('ReceiveTime')]
    raw_event = row[header.index('RawMessage')]
    event = Event(raw_event)
    event.timestamp = datetime.strptime(timestamp, TIME_FMT)
    events.append(event)
  return sorted(events, key=lambda x: (x.user, x.timestamp))
```

The code snippet above normalizes the data from the VPN logs. We normalize the data because VPN logs, as most logs, are typically unstructured text similar to the one listed below.

```
<164>%ASA-4-722051: Group < VPN_GROUP_POLICY>

User < user1> IP <108.178.181.38> Address <10.10.10.10> assigned to
session
```

Typically, if you would want to analyze data, you would want to process it so that it can be in a usable format. We use the normalize() method to do just that. In our case, we would like to structure our data so that we are able to separate the data into the following elements:

- the User ID,
- the external IP address,
- the internal IP address, and
- date and time.

Let us go through the code and see what it does:

- The program loads the "ReceiveTime" column and the "RawMessage." We obtained these columns through the reader object via the CSV module.
- Then, the program processes the timestamp to a more usable format. There are certain formats that do not work well in manipulating data. In this case, the format in our VPN logs, such as "Apr 3, 2013 2:05:20 PM HST," is a string conducive to data manipulation (e.g., sorting operations). We used the datetime.strptime() class method to convert the string to an actual date/time format, allowing us to perform date/time manipulation on the data.
- The program passes the "rawmessage" to an Event object. First let us look at the Event class. The Event class looks like the below code:

```
class Event(object):
    """ Basic event class for handling log events """
    _rules = []
    _rules.append(Rule('ASA-4-722051', 'connect', CONNECT))
    _rules.append(Rule('ASA-5-722037', 'disconnect', DISCONNECT))

    def __init__(self, raw_event):
        for rule in self._rules:
            if rule.key in raw_event:
                self._match_rule(rule, raw_event)
                self.key = rule.title

    def _match_rule(self, rule, raw_event):
        match = rule.regex.match(raw_event)
        for key, value in match.groupdict().iteritems():
            setattr(self, key, value)

    def __str__(self):
        return str(self.__dict__)

    def __repr__(self):
        return repr(self.__dict__)
```

The Event class then utilizes the Rule class, which looks like the following:

```python
class Rule(object):
    """ Basic rule object class """
    def __init__(self, key, title, regex):
        self.key = key
        self.title = title
        self.regex = re.compile(regex)
```

- What do the Event and Rule classes do? Basically, these functions are used to parse the VPN logs into "structured" events. This is done via the "Rules" class that uses regular expressions to break down the string. For example, "connect" events in the VPN logs are parsed using this command:

```python
CONNECT = (r'.*> User <(?P<user>.*)> IP<(?P<external>.*)> '
r'Address <(?P<internal>.*)> assigned to session')
```

- If you look at the command above, using the regular expression inside the CONNECT variable, the program will be able to extract the user, the external IP, and internal IP information from the raw message of the VPN log.
- Finally, once we have parsed and normalized all the needed information, we sort the events based on users and timestamp. By doing this, we will be able to compare the following:
  - when and where the user is currently logged in, and
  - when and where the user previously logged in before the current login.

The reason for this will be more readily apparent as we go through the analysis of the data.

Run the Analytics

```python
def analyze(events):
    """ Main event analysis loops """
    gi = GeoIPopen(GEOIP_DB, GeoIP.GEOIP_STANDARD)
    for i, event in enumerate(events):
        # calculate the geoip information
        if event.external:
            record = gi.record_by_addr(event.external)
            events[i].geoip_cc = record['country_code']
            events[i].geoip_lat = record['latitude']
            events[i].geoip_long = record['longitude']
        # calculate the haversine distance
        if i > 0:
            if events[i].user == events[i-1].user:
                origin = (events[i-1].geoip_lat, events[i-1].geoip_long)
```

```
                destination = (events[i].geoip_lat, events[i].geoip_
                long)
                events[i].haversine = distance(origin, destination)
            else:
                events[i].haversine = 0.0
        else:
            events[i].haversine = 0.0
    return events
```

This is the "meat" of the script we are creating. This is where we compute the haversine distance we will be using to detect unusual VPN connections. First, we need to get the location. We do this by identifying the location of the connection and utilizing the MaxMind GeoIP API:

```
gi = GeoIP.open(GEOIP_DB, GeoIP.GEOIP_STANDARD)
for i, event in enumerate(events):
    # calculate the geoip information
    if event.external:
        record = gi.record_by_addr(event.external)
        events[i].geoip_cc = record['country_code']
        events[i].geoip_lat = record['latitude']
        events[i].geoip_long = record['longitude']
```

Here you see that we create a GeoIP object. Then, we go through all the events and pass the external IP address (using event.external) to get the following GeoIP information:

- country code,
- latitude, and
- longitude.

The latitude and longitude are the essential elements we need to compute the haversine distance here:

```
# calculate the haversine distance
if i > 0:
    if events[i].user == events[i-1].user:
        origin = (events[i-1].geoip_lat, events[i-1].geoip_long)
        destination = (events[i].geoip_lat, events[i].geoip_long)
        events[i].haversine = distance(origin, destination)
    else:
        events[i].haversine = 0.0
else:
    events[i].haversine = 0.0
```

We compare before and after connections for one user in this section. Here is the pseudocode on how the code operates:

- Is the previous event from the same user?
- If yes, then:
  - Where did the user's current connection come from?

- Where did the connection before this current one come from?
- Compute for the haversine distance
- If no, then:
  - Zero out the haversine computation.

Pretty simple, is it not? So now, how is the haversine distance computed? The distance method in the code is used:

```
def distance(origin, destination):
    """ Haversine distance calculation
    https://gist.github.com/rochacbruno/2883505</u>
    """
    lat1, lon1 = origin
    lat2, lon2 = destination
    radius = 6371 # km
    dlat = math.radians(lat2-lat1)
    dlon = math.radians(lon2-lon1)
    a = math.sin(dlat/2) * math.sin(dlat/2) +
math.cos(math.radians(lat1)) \
        * math.cos(math.radians(lat2)) * math.sin(dlon/2) * math.
        sin(dlon/2)
    c = 2 * math.atan2(math.sqrt(a), math.sqrt(1-a))
    d = radius * c
    return d
```

This is a little bit hard to explain without teaching you math, so we will not be covering these details in this book. The important thing for you to know about the code here is the technique we are using and we know how to use Google!

In this case, a simple search for "Havesine Python" would lead you to a ton of resources. We are crediting Waybe Dyck for a piece of code made available in Github for the haversine calculation. And, that is the code we will be using! It is now time to run it and analyze the results.

ANALYZING THE RESULTS

To run the code, all you really need to do is to type in the following command:

```
python analyze.py vpn.csv -o out.csv
```

When the program is run, it will do the following:

- Load the VPN log information from vpn.csv
- The program will run the analytics we discussed in the previous section
- The program will then write the results in a file called out.csv file

Let us open up the vpn.csv file in a spreadsheet and look at the results. The results should look like something similar to the following (Figure 5.3):

timestamp	user	external	reason	geoip_cc	geoip_lat	geoip_lon	haversine
4/3/13 9:12	user1	67.53.40.236		US	21.3209	-157.8389	0
4/3/13 9:15	user1	67.53.40.236	User Request	US	21.3209	-157.8389	0
4/3/13 9:47	user1	67.53.40.236		US	21.3209	-157.8389	0
4/3/13 9:49	user1	67.53.40.236	User Request	US	21.3209	-157.8389	0
4/1/13 16:43	user2	72.234.151.233		US	19.4601002	-155.0246	0
4/1/13 18:17	user2	72.234.151.233	User Request	US	19.4601002	-155.0246	0
4/1/13 20:49	user2	72.234.151.233		US	19.4601002	-155.0246	0
4/1/13 22:46	user2	72.234.151.233	User Request	US	19.4601002	-155.0246	0
4/2/13 23:22	user3	75.85.132.182		US	21.4701004	-157.9637	0
4/3/13 1:56	user3	75.85.132.182	DPD failure.	US	21.4701004	-157.9637	0
4/3/13 1:57	user3	75.85.132.182	DPD failure.	US	21.4701004	-157.9637	0
3/30/13 23:40	user4	50.113.7.155		US	21.3421993	-157.8374	0
3/31/13 0:42	user4	50.113.7.155	User Request	US	21.3421993	-157.8374	0
4/1/13 10:40	user4	50.113.7.155		US	21.3421993	-157.8374	0
4/1/13 12:27	user4	50.113.7.155	User Request	US	21.3421993	-157.8374	0
3/27/13 16:27	user5	12.226.166.178		US	33.2229996	-117.1069	0
3/27/13 16:45	user5	12.226.166.178	User Request	US	33.2229996	-117.1069	0
3/28/13 18:43	user5	12.226.166.178		US	33.2229996	-117.1069	0
3/28/13 19:26	user5	12.226.166.178	User Request	US	33.2229996	-117.1069	0
3/31/13 17:30	user5	12.226.166.178		US	33.2229996	-117.1069	0
3/31/13 17:40	user5	12.226.166.178	User Request	US	33.2229996	-117.1069	0
3/27/13 16:03	user6	70.199.227.232		US	45.5233994	-122.6762	0
3/28/13 10:39	user6	70.199.227.232	Transport clc	US	45.5233994	-122.6762	0
3/28/13 14:08	user6	70.199.224.111		US	45.5233994	-122.6762	0
3/28/13 16:20	user6	70.199.224.111	Transport clc	US	45.5233994	-122.6762	0
4/3/13 9:09	user6	70.199.228.226		US	45.5233994	-122.6762	0
3/27/13 22:21	user7	76.88.137.124		US	21.3267002	-157.8167	0
3/28/13 1:08	user7	76.88.137.124		US	21.3267002	-157.8167	0
3/28/13 2:23	user7	76.88.137.124	Transport clc	US	21.3267002	-157.8167	0
3/28/13 22:16	user8	76.93.194.140		US	21.3775005	-158.0862	0
3/28/13 22:46	user8	76.93.194.140	User Request	US	21.3775005	-158.0862	0
3/29/13 19:07	user8	24.43.224.194		US	24.8598003	-168.0218	1086.93909
3/29/13 20:02	user8	24.43.224.194	DPD failure.	US	24.8598003	-168.0218	0
3/29/13 20:04	user8	24.43.224.194	DPD failure.	US	24.8598003	-168.0218	0
3/31/13 19:23	user8	76.93.194.140		US	21.3775005	-158.0862	1086.93909
3/31/13 22:21	user8	76.93.194.140	Transport clc	US	21.3775005	-158.0862	0
3/28/13 10:38	user9	98.150.159.172		US	21.2982998	-157.7919	0
3/28/13 12:26	user9	98.150.159.172	User Request	US	21.2982998	-157.7919	0
3/29/13 8:56	user9	98.150.159.172		US	21.2982998	-157.7919	0
3/29/13 13:41	user9	98.150.159.172	User Request	US	21.2982998	-157.7919	0
3/29/13 15:04	user9	98.150.159.172		US	21.2982998	-157.7919	0

FIGURE 5.3

Sample output of the remote access script.

The important information here is the last column, containing the haversine distance. This should be the focus of your review. We want to look for the larger haversine distance because it means the locations between the logins are greater. Therefore, the greater the haversine distance, the more suspicious it is.

3/28/13 2:23	user7	76.88.137.124	Transport clc	US	21.3267002	-157.8167	0
3/28/13 22:16	user8	76.93.194.140		US	21.3775005	-158.0862	0
3/28/13 22:46	user8	76.93.194.140	User Reques	US	21.3775005	-158.0862	0
3/29/13 19:07	user8	24.43.224.194		US	24.8598003	-168.0218	1086.93909
3/29/13 20:02	user8	24.43.224.194	DPD failure.	US	24.8598003	-168.0218	0
3/29/13 20:04	user8	24.43.224.194	DPD failure.	US	24.8598003	-168.0218	0
3/31/13 19:23	user8	76.93.194.140		US	21.3775005	-158.0862	1086.93909
3/31/13 22·21	user8	76 93 194 140	Transport clc	US	21 3775005	-158 0862	0

FIGURE 5.4

Reviewing the access behavior of User8.

Let us go through some examples to make it clearer. First off, here are some quick guidelines in doing the review:

- Disregard haversine distances that are 0.
- Look for haversine distances that are large (e.g., greater that 1000). This is generally up to your discretion, but most of it is common sense. For example, let us look at "user8" (Figure 5.4):

User8 has a fairly large haversine distance. If you do a GeoIP lookup, for example, using http://www.geoiptool.com, it shows that the connections are coming from the same state (Hawaii) but in different towns. You can also see that the date is one day apart, so it is not as suspicious at it seems. But, based on your level of tolerance, you can develop a policy to call and verify if a user's login was valid for that day.

- Let us look for larger haversine distances in the list. You will see some that are fairly large such as this one for "user90." (Figure 5.5)

There are several fairly large haversine distances here. If you use a GeoIP locator, you will be able to piece together the connection behavior of this user:

- 64.134.237.89 (Hawaii)
- 66.175.72.33 (California)
- 64.134.237.89 (Hawaii)
- 66.175.72.33 (California)

Note that this is in the span of one day. Actually, the first three logins were in the span of a couple of hours. This is obviously something worth investigating and, at the very least, having a security officer question user90 about these logins. Of course, this does not automatically mean that the connections are malicious. There could be valid reasons causing a user to connect through remote machines. In any case, this is something worth investigating.

4/1/13 22:15	user90	76.93.217.150	US	21.3267002	-157.8167	2.3884208
4/1/13 22:53	user90	76.93.217.150	US	21.3267002	-157.8167	0
4/2/13 11:26	user90	66.175.72.33	US	21.3209	-157.8389	2.3884208
4/2/13 12:10	user90	66.175.72.33	US	21.3209	-157.8389	0
4/2/13 13:05	user90	108.178.181.38	US	21.3136005	-157.80569	3.53389091
4/2/13 13:56	user90	108.178.181.38	US	21.3136005	-157.80569	0
4/2/13 15:48	user90	66.175.72.33	US	21.3209	-157.8389	3.53389091
4/2/13 16:06	user90	64.134.237.89	US	34.0522003	-118.2437	4117.41858
4/2/13 16:59	user90	66.175.72.33	US	21.3209	-157.8389	4117.41858
4/2/13 17:15	user90	64.134.237.89	US	34.0522003	-118.2437	4117.41858
4/3/13 9:17	user90	66.175.72.33	US	21.3209	-157.8389	4117.41858
4/3/13 10:42	user90	66.175.72.33	US	21.3209	-157.8389	0
4/3/13 12:33	user90	66.175.72.33	US	21.3209	-157.8389	0
4/3/13 13:28	user90	66.175.72.33	US	21.3209	-157.8389	0
4/3/13 14:05	user90	108.178.181.38	US	21.3136005	-157.80569	3.53389091

FIGURE 5.5
Reviewing the access behavior of User90.

4/1/13 11:16	user91	66.175.72.33	US	21.3209	-157.8389	0
4/1/13 11:48	user91	66.175.72.33	US	21.3209	-157.8389	0
4/1/13 21:23	user91	72.235.23.189	US	21.3469009	-158.0183	18.804763
4/2/13 9:08	user91	72.235.23.189	US	21.3469009	-158.0183	0
4/2/13 9:09	user91	72.235.23.189	US	21.3469009	-158.0183	0
4/2/13 17:09	user91	72.235.23.189	US	21.3469009	-158.0183	0
4/3/13 6:29	user91	72.235.23.189	US	21.3469009	-158.0183	0
4/3/13 10:20	user91	198.23.71.73	US	32.9299011	-96.835297	6106.99523
4/3/13 10:20	user91	198.23.71.73	US	32.9299011	-96.835297	0
4/3/13 11:21	user91	198.23.71.73	US	32.9299011	-96.835297	0
4/3/13 13:45	user91	66.175.72.33	US	21.3209	-157.8389	6091.56662

FIGURE 5.6
Reviewing the access behavior of User91.

Let us look another one (Figure 5.6). This one has an even bigger haversine distance:

If we investigate this further, we see this connection behavior in the span of one day:

- 72.235.23.189 (Hawaii)
- 198.23.71.73 (Texas)
- 198.23.71.73 (Texas)
- 198.23.71.73 (Texas)
- 66.175.72.33 (Hawaii)

As we already discussed, since these connections happened in a span of a few hours, this is not an absolute indication of a malicious connection. Plausible reasons for these types of connections include the following:

- The user is connecting through a remote machine.
- The user is using some sort of proxy or mobile service.
- Some users are sharing accounts.
- The account is compromised and a malicious user is connecting as the user.

In any of these scenarios, it is worthwhile to verify if these are valid connections. Ultimately, this type of review can be incorporated as a regular remote access review program, whereby the goal is to identify potentially malicious remote connections. Aside from checking for haversine distances, you could use the script as a foundation for creating other analysis methods to identify other misuse of remote access connections. You could consider expanding your script by including the following:

- concurrent connection of the same user,
- concurrent users,
- connection between two times,
- connections from certain countries,
- connections greater than x amounts per day,
- user connects in unusual times,
- user connects from unusual locations,
- the frequency of connections, and many more...

The principles discussed here can also be applied to other data sets. For example, this technique can be utilized for examining server or database access logs. The scripts can be easily tweaked to review physical access logs, as well such for identifying physical access into facilities at unusual times or frequencies.

Security and Text Mining

SCENARIOS AND CHALLENGES IN SECURITY ANALYTICS WITH TEXT MINING

Massive amounts of unstructured data are being collected from online sources, such as e-mails, call center transcripts, wikis, online bulletin boards, blogs, tweets, Web pages, and so on. Also, as noted in a previous chapter, large amounts of data are also being collected in semistructured form, such as log files containing information from servers and networks. Semistructured data sets are not quite as free form as the body of an e-mail, but are not as rigidly structured as tables and columns in a relational database. Text mining analysis is useful for both unstructured and semistructured textual data.

There are many ways that text mining can be used for security analytics. E-mails can be analyzed to discover patterns in words and phrases, which may indicate a phishing attack. Call center recordings can be converted to text, which then can be analyzed to find patterns and phrases, which may indicate attempts to use a stolen identity, gain passwords to secure systems, or commit other fraudulent acts. Web sites can be scraped and analyzed to find trends in security-related themes, such as the latest botnet threats, malware, and other Internet hazards.

There has been a proliferation of new tools available to deal with the challenge of analyzing unstructured, textual data. While there are many commercial tools available, often with significant costs to purchase them, some tools are free and open source. We will focus on open source tools in this chapter. This is not to say, of course, that the commercial tools offer less value. Many offer significant ease of use advantages, and come with a wide array of analytical methods. In some cases, the benefits may outweigh the costs. Open source software tools, however, can be accessed by most readers regardless of budget constraints, and are useful for learning about text mining analysis methods in general.

Popular open source software for analyzing small- to moderate-sized bodies of text includes R, Python, and Weka. In the case of Big Data, popular tools used to mine for relationships in text include Hadoop/MapReduce, Mahout, Hive, and Pig, to name a few. Since R has a particularly comprehensive set of text mining tools available in a package called "tm," we will mainly focus on R for this chapter. The "tm" package can be downloaded from the CRAN repository, at www.cran.r-project.org.

USE OF TEXT MINING TECHNIQUES TO ANALYZE AND FIND PATTERNS IN UNSTRUCTURED DATA

The phrase, text mining, refers to the process of analyzing textual data, to find hidden relationships between important themes. Regardless of the toolsets or languages used, there are methods used in text mining that are common to all. This section provides a brief description of some of the more common text mining methods and data transformations. However, it is not meant to be a comprehensive coverage of the topic. Rather, these concepts cover some of the basics required to follow the examples provided later in this chapter.

Text Mining Basics

In order to analyze textual data with computers, it is necessary to convert it from text to numbers. The most basic means of accomplishing this is by counting the number of times that certain words appear within a document. The result is generally a table, or matrix of word frequencies.

A common way to represent word frequencies in a table is to have each column represent a single word that appears in any one of a collection of documents. This arrangement is known as a "document-term matrix." It is also possible to transpose the matrix, so that each document name becomes a column header and each row represents a different word. This arrangement is called a "term document matrix." For our example later in this chapter, we will focus on the document-term matrix format, with each column representing a word.

Each unique word heading in a column can be referred to as a "term," "token," or simply "word," interchangeably. This can be confusing to text mining newcomers. But just remember that "term," and "token," merely refer to a single representation of a word.

Each row in the document-term matrix table represents a single document. For instance, a row might represent a single blog with other rows in the table representing other blogs.

The numerical values within the body of the table represent the number of times each word appears in a given document. There may be many terms that appear in only one document or just a few documents. These frequency numbers can be further transformed to account for such things as differences in document sizes, reducing words to their root forms, and inversely weighting the frequencies by how commonly certain words appear within a given language.

Common Data Transformations for Text Mining

Text data is notoriously messy. Many of the common data transformations used in text mining do nothing more than make the data analyzable. For instance, text often contains extra characters that are generally meaningless for analyzing word frequencies. These characters, and even extra white space, all must be removed.

Some of the most frequently occurring words in any language are also meaningless for most kinds of analysis and must be removed. These words are collected in a "stop word list," also known as a "stop word corpus." This list commonly includes words such as "the," "of," "a," "is," "be," and hundreds of others that, while frequently appearing in documents, are not very interesting for most text mining projects. Computers can compare the words that appear in documents, to a stop word list. Only those words that do not appear in the stop word list will be included in the word frequency table.

STEP BY STEP TEXT MINING EXAMPLE IN R

For our example, suppose we wish to know common themes in reported system vulnerabilities in the Web Hacking Incident Database (WHID), maintained by the Web Application Security Consortium, at webappsec.org. This database is convenient for illustration purposes, due to its moderate size, and ease of data collection. The database Web site offers users the ability to download data in CSV format, making it easy to import into R, or almost any other text mining software for analysis. The complete URL from which these sample data sets were retrieved is: https://www.google.com/fusiontables/DataSource?snapid=S195929w1ly.

The data consists of 19 columns. Following is a complete list of all the column headings.

- "EntryTitle"
- "WHIDID"
- "DateOccured"
- "AttackMethod"
- "ApplicationWeakness"
- "Outcome"
- "AttackedEntityField"
- "AttackedEntityGeography"
- "IncidentDescription"
- "MassAttack"
- "MassAttackName"
- "NumberOfSitesAffected"
- "Reference"
- "AttackSourceGeography"
- "AttackedSystemTechnology"
- "Cost"
- "ItemsLeaked"
- "NumberOfRecords"
- "AdditionalLink"

For the purpose illustration, we will focus on two columns: "DateOccurred" and "IncidentDescription." These are columns 3 and 9, respectively. Note, that for the purpose of analysis, we removed the spaces from the column names. Spaces in column names can create problems with some analytical algorithms. If you wish to download your own data set to follow along with this analysis, you will need to remove the spaces so that the column names appear exactly as appearing in the preceding list.

Most of our R code will be devoted to the IncidentDescription column, since that is where the bulk of the text exists. This column contains highly detailed narratives pertaining to each incident. Each description can be as much as a couple hundred words or more, providing more to text to analyze than any other column in the data set. Text analysis could also be performed on other columns as well, and might even reveal some interesting relationships between different column variables. However, by focusing on the "IncidentDescription" column, we will keep this analysis as simple as possible to serve as an introduction to basic text mining methods and techniques.

R Code Walk-through

The first line in our R code example removes any objects that might have already existed in your R environment. If you are running the code for the first time, this step will not be necessary. But, it will not hurt anything to include it, either. When developing code, you may find yourself modifying and rerunning code sets over again. For this reason, you will want to be sure there are no unwanted remnant variable values or other objects remaining in your R environment, before you run your code anew.

Initiating the Package Libraries and Importing the Data

```
rm(list=ls()) #Start with a clean slate: remove all objects
```

Next, we load all the libraries needed for our analysis. Recall that the "#" symbol denotes comments. The code is liberally commented to improve understanding as to what the code does.

```
#Load libraries
library(tm) #for text mining functions
library(corrplot) #for creating plots of correlation matrices
```

The "tm" package contains many more functions than we can cover in a single chapter. They are worth exploring, however. A full index of all the available functions within this package can be produced in R, with the following command.

```
#See tm package documentation and index of functions
library(help=tm)
```

Now, we can import the data from the CSV file, using R's "read.csv" function. We set the header parameter to a value of TRUE, since the first row of the CSV file contains the headers. The next line of code then takes the imported data and converts it to a text corpus. The "corpus" function extracts the text data from the column we specify, which is "IncidentDescription," in this case. The function also includes metadata that is necessary for the text mining functions we will be applying later in the analysis.

```
rawData <- read.csv("DefaultWHIDView2.csv",header=TRUE)
data <- Corpus(VectorSource(rawData[,"IncidentDescription"]))
```

Text Data Cleansing

At this point, we are ready to begin applying data transformations that will clean up the text and put it into an analyzable format. Here, we use a variety functions in the "tm" package. The "tm_map" function maps a specified transformation to the text data. This function allows us to specify a nested transformation function.

The first use of the "tm_map" function calls the "stripWhitespace" function from within it. As the function's name implies, this combination will strip all white space from the text.

The second tm_map function calls a data cleansing function called, "stemDocument." This function combination will reduce all words to their root forms.

For example, the terms "reading," and "reads" would be converted to the stem word, "read," which can also be referred to as a root word. This can be a handy transformation, depending upon the objective of your analysis. However, the transformation can also create some problems as well. Sometimes the extra characters after a stem word are not superfluous after all. They can, in some cases, completely change the meaning of a word. You should experiment with your own text data, to see how stemming affects your results. In the case of the data for this example, the results appear valid for the most part, without the use of stemming. Thus, the stemming step is commented out in the code, but is left for reference purposes.

The next line uses the "toLower" function. This also is self-explanatory, as it simply changes all the letters to lowercase.

At this point in the code, we assemble a list of stopwords, using the "stop-words" function in the "tm" package. Notice the parameter, "english," which specifies a list of stopwords for the English language. There are other languages that are supported by this function as well. See the function's built-in help for other language parameters that can be used. Recall that help for a function can be called by simply typing a question mark in front of the function name, such as "?stopwords." Running the stopwords function returns a vector of stop-words, and we assign this list of stopwords to a variable we also are calling "stopWords." On the next line of code, the "stopWords" variable is used to provide a list to the "removewords" function, which is embedded within the tm_map function. This removes all words that appear in the "stopWords" list from the text corpus. (Note that corpus just means "body." So, "text corpus" is the same as "text body.")

The last two lines in the code section remove all punctuation and numerals from the text. They utilize the functions, "removePunctuation" and "removeNumbers," respectively.

```
#Cleanup text
data2 = tm_map(data, stripWhitespace)
#data2 = tm_map(data2, stemDocument)
data2 = tm_map(data2, tolower)
stopWords = c(stopwords("english"))
data2 = tm_map(data2, removeWords, stopWords)
data2 = tm_map(data2, removePunctuation)
data2 = tm_map(data2, removeNumbers)
```

Let's review a sample of what all this data cleansing has done to our text. To do this, we use the "inspect" function. Notice how the results maintain the individual documents and their index numbers. Only the first two documents are shown here to save space. The results also begin with a brief metadata description. Metadata are sometimes described as simply being "data about the data."

```
> inspect(data2[1:5])
A corpus with 5 text documents
The metadata consists of 2 tag-value pairs and a data frame.
Available tags are:
create_date creator
Available variables in the data frame are:
MetaID

[[1]]
department health hospitals spokeswoman lisa faust said bureau
emergency medical services personnel discovered database breach
unauthorized entry gave hacker access individuals name personal
information including social security numbers dont know whether
hacker able access information faust said computer screen displayed
message hacked faust said since dont know one way sent notices peo-
ple s potential information compromised wasc whid note portal login
page httpsemsophdhhlagovemsloginasp looks vulnerable sql injection

[[2]]
boingboingnet popular blog directory wonderful things hacked home
page replaced message containing vulgar language pictures site
pulled administrators shortly attack suspected executed via sql
injection techcrunch reports
```

Creating a Document-Term Matrix

Now that we have cleaned up the text, we are ready to convert it into a word
frequency matrix. We will use the document-term matrix format, which lists
the words, or tokens, as column headers, and each document as a separate row.
The number of times each token appears within a document is given at the
intersection between a row number and a token column heading.

We use the "DocumentTermMatrix" function to create the matrix, and assign
the results to a variable we are calling, "dtm." Lastly, we inspect the first five
rows and the first five columns using the "inspect" function. Notice how the
results give the metadata for the matrix. The metadata description says that
there are no nonsparse entries. This means that all five of the returned terms
have zero entries in the five documents shown. If we wanted to see a value
returned for these, we would have to view more than just five entries.

```
> #Make a word frequency matrix, with documents as rows, and terms
as columns
> dtm = DocumentTermMatrix(data2)
> inspect(dtm[1:5,1:5])
A document-term matrix (5 documents, 5 terms)
Non-/sparse entries: 0/25
Sparsity: 100%
Maximal term length: 10
Weighting: term frequency (tf)
```

```
Terms
Docs aapl abandoned abc abcnewscom abell
1 0 0 0 0 0
2 0 0 0 0 0
3 0 0 0 0 0
4 0 0 0 0 0
5 0 0 0 0 0
```

Removing Sparse Terms

It is common in text mining to see many terms that only appear in a few documents or sometimes even one document. These are called sparse entries. In the next code sample, we will remove sparse terms from our document-term matrix using the "removeSparseTerms" function. This function has a parameter for setting a percentage threshold. Any words that are above this sparse threshold will be removed. In this case, we set the threshold to "0.90," which is 90%. Note that you must type the percentage as a decimal. You should experiment with different thresholds to see what produces the best results for your analysis. If the threshold is set too high, your results may contain too many isolated terms and will not reveal any significant patterns. However, set the threshold too low and you could end up removing words that have significant meaning. Lastly, we inspected the first five rows and columns, and can see some frequency numbers appearing, now that many of the most sparse terms have been removed.

```
> #Remove and sparse terms a given percentage of sparse (i.e., 0)
occurence
> dtm = removeSparseTerms(dtm, 0.90)
> inspect(dtm[1:5,1:5])
A document-term matrix (5 documents, 5 terms)

Non-/sparse entries: 6/19
Sparsity: 76%
Maximal term length: 6
Weighting: term frequency (tf)

Terms
Docs access attack can data hacked
1 2 0 0 0 1
2 0 1 0 0 1
3 0 0 0 0 0
4 0 2 0 0 0
5 0 1 0 0 0
```

Data Profiling with Summary Statistics

Now that the data set has been cleansed and transformed, and we have a document-term matrix in hand, we are ready to begin some analysis. One of the first things you should be in the habit of doing with any kind of data analysis is to look at a data profile. A data profile contains descriptive statistics that help give you a feel for your data. It is a great way of giving your data a reasonableness check and look for possible anomalies. R makes it easy to get descriptive statistics, using a standard function called "summary." Descriptive statistics produced by this function include minimum, maximum, mean, and median, as well as the first and third quartiles. These can really help you to understand the shape of the distribution your data.

Notice that we are embedding the "inspect" function within the "summary" function. This is necessary, since the document-term matrix, "dtm," uses text corpus data. As noted earlier, a text corpus includes metadata required for a number of text analytical functions in the "tm" package. The "inspect" function separates the plain frequency data from the metadata. In other words, it returns a data frame table type, which is what is required of the summary function. Any time you may want to use a standard R function, other than a function within the "tm" package, you will likely need to use the "inspect" function in a similar manner, since most standard R functions require a data frame format, rather than a text corpus format. Notice also, that within the "inspect" function, we have used R's indexing functionality, by specifying within square brackets that we only want the first three columns returned.

The result indicates that these first three terms are still fairly sparse. For instance, the word "access" appears an average of 14% of the time among all documents, with a maximum frequency of four occurrences in a single document.

```
summary(inspect(dtm[,1:3]))
access attack can
Min.:0.0000 Min.:0.0000 Min.:0.0000
1st Qu.:0.0000 1st Qu.:0.0000 1st Qu.:0.0000
Median:0.0000 Median:0.0000 Median:0.0000
Mean:0.1403 Mean:0.3073 Mean:0.1332
3rd Qu.:0.0000 3rd Qu.:0.0000 3rd Qu.:0.0000
Max.:4.0000 Max.:8.0000 Max.:4.0000
```

Finding Commonly Occurring Terms

One of the more common things we want to do in text analysis, is to determine which terms appear most frequently. The "findFreqTerms" function within the "tm" package is useful for this purpose. This function has a parameter that sets a threshold for a minimum frequency. Only words that have at least this level of frequency or more will be returned by the function. This example sets the threshold at 100, since this reduces the list to something more printable in a book.

Notice in the output from this function that there is an odd word appearing as "ppadditional." This is an anomaly in the data that is the result of the fact that the original data had some HTML tags that crept into the CSV file. In this case, a pair of paragraph tags denoted as "<p>" in the text. When you find such anomalies, you will need to determine whether it affects your analysis enough to be worthwhile spend the extra effort to clean them up. In this case, as we will see later, the impact of this anomaly is inconsequential and easy to spot.

```
> #Find terms that occur at least n times
> findFreqTerms(dtm, 100)
[1] "attack" "hacked" "hacker" "hackers"
[5] "information" "informationp" "injection" "one"
[9] "ppadditional" "security" "site" "sites"
[13] "sql" "used" "vulnerability" "web"
[17] "website"
```

Word Associations

Often, we maybe interested in knowing whether there are any terms associated with a particular word theme. In other words, we want to know which terms in our collection of documents may be correlated with a given term. The "tm" package's "findAssocs" function can help us with this. In the example below, we give the "findAssocs" function three parameters: (1) the object containing the data-term matrix or "dtm" in this case; (2) the word for which we want to find associated terms, which is the word, "attack" in this example; and (3) the correlation threshold, also referred to as an r-value, or 0.1 in this case. There are no hard fast rules for setting the correlation threshold. This one is set very low to include more associated words in the result. However, if your document has many associated words in it, you might set this threshold much higher to reduce the number of words returned by the function. It is a subjective, iterative process to find the balance you need for your analysis.

In the output for this function, notice there were eight words returned that at least met the correlation threshold. Their respective correlation values are showing in a vector of numbers. In this case, the word "attack" is most closely associated with the word "injection." This, no doubt, refers to the use of the phrase "injection attack," which refers to a means of injecting malicious commands into a system, such as by SQL injection into a database. Notice that "sql" is the second most associated term. Next in line for the commonly referred to terms are "sites" and "service." This most likely refers to reports of SQL injection against Web sites and web services.

```
> findAssocs(dtm, "attack", 0.1)
attack
injection 0.30
sql 0.29
sites 0.24
service 0.23
access 0.16
```

```
incident 0.12
new 0.10
web 0.10
```

Transposing the Term Matrix

At this point, it might be interesting to see whether our results for the above word association exercise might have changed, had we elected to transpose our matrix to a term document matrix, instead of a document-term matrix. In other words, what if the columns represented documents instead of words and the rows represented words instead of documents? Notice that we store the resulting matrix in a variable called "tdm" for "term-document matrix" to compare against the variable "dtm" for "document-term matrix."

Running the code below, we can see that it makes no difference in this case. All the preceding steps for the document-term matrix were repeated here, only the data are transposed. If we had far more documents than words, and we wished to focus on the words, we might find it more convenient to transpose our matrix in this way.

```
> inspect(tdm[1:5,1:5])
A term-document matrix (5 terms, 5 documents)

Non-/sparse entries: 0/25
Sparsity: 100%
Maximal term length: 10
Weighting: term frequency (tf)

Docs
Terms 1 2 3 4 5
aapl 0 0 0 0 0
abandoned 0 0 0 0 0
abc 0 0 0 0 0
abcnewscom 0 0 0 0 0
abell 0 0 0 0 0
>
> tdm = removeSparseTerms(tdm, 0.90)
> inspect(tdm[1:5,1:5])
A term-document matrix (5 terms, 5 documents)

Non-/sparse entries: 6/19
Sparsity: 76%
Maximal term length: 6
Weighting: term frequency (tf)

Docs
Terms 1 2 3 4 5
access 2 0 0 0 0
attack 0 1 0 2 1
can 0 0 0 0 0
data 0 0 0 0 0
```

```
hacked 1 1 0 0 0
>
> findAssocs(tdm, "attack", 0.1)
attack
injection 0.30
sql 0.29
sites 0.24
service 0.23
access 0.16
incident 0.12
new 0.10
web 0.10
```

As we see from the above, the most associated terms along with their respective correlations are exactly the same in this transposed matrix, as with the original term document matrix.

Trends over Time

Earlier, we said that we wanted to see if there were any patterns in the text over time. We will now convert the "DateOccured" (sic) column from a string format, to a date format, from which we can extract year and month elements. For this example, we will analyze the trends in the usage of key terms by year.

For this conversion, we use the standard R function "as.Date." We use square bracket indexing to identify the date column and use the actual name of the column "DateOccured" (sic). Alternatively, we could have used a number for the index instead of the name. That is, we could have shown it as raw-Data[,3], instead of rawData[,"DateOccured"]. Also, the empty space before the comma within the index brackets refers to the row index, and it means that we want to return all rows. The "as.Date" function also requires a date format string to specify the native format in which the date appears within the data. In this case, the date is in numeric format, with one to two digits given for the month and day, and four digits for the year, with each element separated by a forward slash. For instance, a typical date in the source data appears in the structure, 10/12/2010. We specify the format as "%m/%d/%Y," where the lower case "m" coupled with the percent sign means a single or double digit month, and likewise with %d for the day. The capital "Y" in %Y refers to a four digit year.

Once we have our dates converted to a date object, stored in the variable, "dateVector", we can use the "month" function to extract the months from the date vector and the "year" function to extract the years.

```
> #Convert to date format
> dateVector <- as.Date(rawData[,"DateOccured"], "%m/%d/%Y")
> mnth <- month(dateVector)
> yr <- year(dateVector)
```

Next, we create a data frame by using the standard R "data.frame" function. We add the vectors we created for date, month, and year, to the document-term matrix to create a single table. Notice again, that we used the "inspect" function to retrieve a data frame from within the text corpus object, "dtm."

```
> dtmAndDates <- data.frame(dateVector, mnth,yr,inspect(dtm))
A document-term matrix (563 documents, 30 terms)

Non-/sparse entries: 3039/13851
Sparsity: 82%
Maximal term length: 13
Weighting: term frequency (tf)

Terms
Docs access attack can data hacked hacker hackers...
1 2 0 0 0 1 2 0 0 3
2 0 1 0 0 1 0 0 0 0
3 0 0 0 0 0 2 0 0 0
4 0 2 0 0 0 0 0 0 0
...
> head(dtmAndDates)
dateVector mnth yr access attack can data hacked hacker
1 2010-09-17  9 2010 2 0 0 0 1 2
2 2010-10-27 10 2010 0 1 0 0 1 0
3 2010-10-25 10 2010 0 0 0 0 0 2
4 2010-10-28 10 2010 0 2 0 0 0 0
5 2010-10-27 10 2010 0 1 0 0 0 0
6 2010-10-25 10 2010 0 1 2 0 0 0
```

We see, however, that the results for the daily and even the monthly trends are rather sparse. So, we will make a new data.frame in the same manner that we created the one above, but with data aggregated by years. This will enable us to analyze annual trends in key terms. First, we build a data frame that joins the "yr" vector we created, with the data-term matrix, "dtm," and put the resulting data frame in an object we call "dtmAndYr."

```
> dtmAndYr <- data.frame(yr,inspect(dtm))
A document-term matrix (563 documents, 30 terms)

Non-/sparse entries: 3039/13851
Sparsity: 82%
Maximal term length: 13
Weighting: term frequency (tf)

Terms
Docs access attack can data hacked hacker hackers incident...
1 2 0 0 0 1 2 0 0 3
2 0 1 0 0 1 0 0 0 0
3 0 0 0 0 0 2 0 0 0
```

```
4 0 2 0 0 0 0 0 0 0
5 0 1 0 0 0 0 1 0 0
...
```

Next, we use the standard R function, "aggregate," to sum all the frequencies for each word by year. Notice that we remove the first column from the "dtmAndYr" data frame, by indicating a –1 in the column index place within the square brackets. The first column contains the year value, which would be pointless to sum within the aggregate function, so we remove it from the final result. However, the year column is used for the "by" parameter in the "aggregate" function, as we are summing by year. This point might be confusing, so perhaps we should restate it this way: we are summing by the year, not for the year.

The "by" parameter references the "yr" column by using the dollar sign after the "dtmAndYr" data frame reference, as "dtmAndYr$Yr." This is a standard way that R allows for referencing a single column within a data frame. We could have alternatively referenced this column by using square bracket indexing. But, we use this method here just to show another way it can be done.

Notice also that the "list" function is used to convert the "yr" column to a list format. Otherwise, it would be extracted into a data frame format. R can be very finicky with its unusual data types. In this case the aggregate function requires that the variable that is referenced in its "by" parameter be formatted as a single list.

Lastly, the parentheses that surround the entire line are used to tell R to show the output. Otherwise, without the parentheses, the output would be assigned to the "sumByYear" variable, but would not show in R's output. This works for many functions, but not all. For instance, it will not work for the "rownames" function that we will use in the next section. We will show the output by simply stating the variable name on a line by itself, in that case.

The resulting summations by year indicate that word frequencies have been going up for each year since the WHID began collecting data. This is likely due to a general increase in reporting of attacks overall. The data shown here are truncated to save space. However, the same pattern can be seen to exist for nearly all of the terms. A few exceptions can be noted, however. Although not shown here, the term, "xss," a common abbreviation for a cross-site scripting attack, peaked out in 2006, but has come down significantly since that time. This could be due to the fact that Web sites have tightened their code considerably in more recent years, to prevent these kinds of attacks. Since then, cross site scripting reports seem to have moderated and leveled off.

```
> (sumByYear <- aggregate(dtmAndYr[,-1], by = list(dtmAndYr$yr),
sum))
Group.1 access attack can data hacked hacker...xss
1 2001  0  0  0  0  0  0... 0
```

```
2 2004  0  0  0  0  0  0... 0
3 2005  2  5  0  5 10  4... 9
4 2006  4 12  8  6  6  9...39
5 2007  8 23  8 17 13 24...14
6 2008 10 27  7 14 22 28...11
7 2009  7 27 21 19 10 26... 9
8 2010 42 79 31 17 64 57...11
...
```

Correlation Analysis of Time Series Trends

We might be interested in doing a correlation analysis on these annual trends to see if any particular trend might be related. We cannot correlate the years column, as it is nonnumeric, and it would not make much sense to do this, even if we could. So, we will remove the years column and turn the year labels into row names instead. The correlation function we will be using will not try to correlate years, if they exist only as row names.

We use the "rownames" function to append the years to the data as row headers. Notice the unusual use of this function on the left-hand side of the assignment operator. When the "rownames" function is used by itself, or on the right-hand side of the assignment operator, it returns all the rownames. However, when on the left side of the assignment operator, the "rownames" function will push new row names into the table, as provided on the right-hand side of the assignment operator.

```
> selTermsByYr <- sumByYear[,-1]
> rownames(selTermsByYr) <- sumByYear[,1]
> selTermsByYr
access attack can data hacked hacker hackers incident...
2001  0  0  0  0  0  0  0  0
2004  0  0  0  0  0  0  0  0
2005  2  5  0  5 10  4  3  0
2006  4 12  8  6  6  9  7  6
2007  8 23  8 17 13 24  7 16
2008 10 27  7 14 22 28 17 30
2009  7 27 21 19 10 26 18 35
2010 42 79 31 17 64 57 70 10
...
```

We can now create a correlation matrix on the data by using the "cor" function. Notice again, the use of the surrounding parentheses, so that the output will be shown in the R window, in addition to assigning the resulting matrix to the "corData" variable.

A small sample of the correlation matrix output is shown here. Each value in the matrix represents the correlation coefficient. The closer a value is to 1.0, the more each term is related to each other. The closer a value is to -1.0, the more often one term tends to be absent when the other term is present. The 1.0

values on the diagonal indicate, as we would expect, that each value is perfectly correlated to itself. The matrix is symmetrical, with values mirroring each other on opposite sides of the diagonal. In this sample view, the highest correlation is 0.98, indicating that the trend for the term "attack" is strongly related to the trend for the term "access." This could be an indication of an increase in access attacks, such as through stolen passwords, social hacking in call centers, and so on. Further research would need to be conducted to confirm these hypotheses, of course.

```
> (corData <- cor(selTermsByYr))
access attack can data...
access 1.00000000 0.98036383 0.8619558 0.5848456
attack 0.98036383 1.00000000 0.9226145 0.7270269
can    0.86195584 0.92261449 1.0000000 0.7719258
data   0.58484558 0.72702694 0.7719258 1.0000000
...
```

The entire output from the trends correlation analysis is not only much too large to include here, it would be hard to compare all of the many term correlations even if we could show them. In cases where there are many correlations to examine, it can be helpful to convert the correlation matrix into a graphical image for visualization.

In the code sample that follows, we use the "png" function to start the png image device in R. Then, we run the "corrplot" function. This function generates the visualization, which is converted into an image file by the png image device we just started. Lastly, we turn off the image device, with the function, "dev.off."

```
png("Figure1.png")
corrplot(corData, method="ellipse")
dev.off()
```

The resulting correlation plot can be seen in Figure 6.1. This correlation plot shows the strength of each correlation in two ways: ellipse width, and color shading. The more narrow the ellipse, the more highly correlated the relationship. The more narrow an ellipse, and the more it begins to appear as a straight line, the stronger the correlation. Also, the darker blue shadings indicate a stronger positive relationship. The darker pink shadings indicate a stronger negative correlation. Remember, a negative correlation is not the same as having no correlation. A zero correlation value indicates no correlation. A negative correlation approaching –1 would indicate a strong correlation, where the two variables tend to move in opposite directions. In this case, a negative correlation suggests that when one term is present, the other term tends to be absent.

In Figure 6.1, we can see that some of the strongest correlations occur where terms are commonly used together in a phrase such as "SQL injection." One

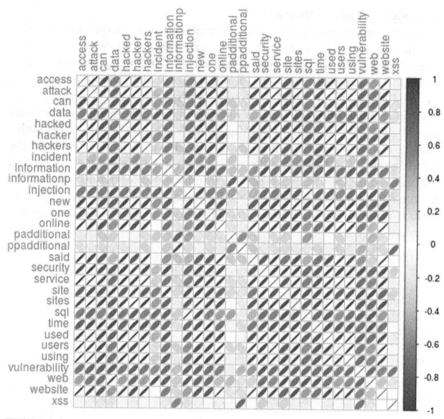

FIGURE 6.1

Visualization of correlation matrix of term frequency trends.

interesting example is the strong positive correlation between the words "attack" and "service." Web services are growing in usage and are increasingly targets of attack. Let's see what terms maybe associated with the term, "service."

```
> #Find associated terms with the term, "service", and a
correlation of at least r
> findAssocs(dtm, "service", 0.1)
service
attack  0.23
hackers 0.12
online  0.11
using   0.10
```

Here we see that terms more commonly associated with the term, "service," include "hackers," "online," and "using," all suggesting usage of online services that got hacked.

Creating a Terms Dictionary

Sometimes, it can be helpful to focus analysis on a select subset of terms that are relevant to the analysis. This can be accomplished through the use of a terms dictionary. In this example, we will use the "dictionary" parameter from within the "DocumentTermMatrix" function. You will recall that this function was used to build our initial document-term matrix. We will again use this function, but will limit the number of terms in it by specifying the dictionary parameter to only include the words, "attack," "security," "site," and "Web." These terms are somewhat arbitrarily chosen. However, they were among the top terms remaining when another analysis, not shown, was done on data that had been reduced with a higher sparsity threshold. Notice in the code, that the dictionary parameter is converted to a list format, by using the "list" function, similar to how we converted the years data frame to a list in an earlier processing step.

```
> #Create a dictionary: a subset of terms
> d = inspect(DocumentTermMatrix(data2, list(dictionary = c("at-
tack", "security", "site", "web"))))
A document-term matrix (563 documents, 4 terms)
Non-/sparse entries: 756/1496
Sparsity: 66%
Maximal term length: 8
Weighting: term frequency (tf)

Terms
Docs attack security site web
1 0 1 0 0
2 1 0 1 0
3 0 0 0 0
4 2 0 1 0
5 1 1 0 0
...
```

We can create a correlation matrix on just these terms, in the same manner as we produced a correlation matrix on the trended data. We see the output below. The only terms that are highly correlated in our dictionary set are "Web," and "site." Of course, these terms are commonly used together to form the phrase, "Web site."

```
> #Correlation matrix
> cor(d) #correlation matrix of dictionary terms only
attack security site web
attack    1.00000000 0.06779848 0.05464950 0.1011398
security 0.06779848 1.00000000 0.06903378 0.1774329
site     0.05464950 0.06903378 1.00000000 0.5582861
web      0.10113977 0.17743286 0.55828610 1.0000000
```

We can create a scatterplot graph to visually inspect any correlations that may appear strong. Sometimes correlations appear due to anomalies, such as outliers. A scatterplot can help us identify these situations. We would not necessarily expect that to be the case in our correlation between "Web" and "site," but we will plot these terms just to demonstrate.

As before, we are using the "png" function to save our graph as a png image. There are similar functions for other image file types including "jpg" and "pdf." They are all set up in the same manner, and all require use of the "dev.off" function to turn the device off after the file is created.

Within the "plot" function, we use another function called "jitter." The "jitter" function adds random noise, to each frequency value, so that we can see how densely each of the frequency values occurs. Otherwise, without adding jitter, every document occurrence of each frequency value would appear as a single point on the graph. For example, there are many documents where the term, "attack," appears only twice. Without adding jitter, all of these documents appear as a single point at the two locations on the axis. Jitter moves, or unstacks these points just enough, so that we can see how many documents share that same value.

You will notice a tilde between the variables in the "plot" function. This tilde is also commonly used in various sorts of regression models, as we will see in the regression function that creates the diagonal line in this graph. You could mentally replace the word "tilde," with the word "by." So, if you are trying to see if a variable, "x," predicts a variable, "y," you would say "y by x," which would be written as "y~x" in the function. Here, we are saying "site by Web." It would reverse the order of the axes, if we replaced the tilde with a comma. This could be done, but the result would not be consistent with the order of the variables we used in the regression function, "lm," that follows. More will be discussed on the "lm" function in a moment.

We can see in the scatterplot output in Figure 6.2, that co-occurrences of "Web" and "site" are indeed correlated, as indicated by the general diagonal shape of all the points, from the bottom left corner, toward the upper right corner. We can also see from the jitter that higher frequencies of co-occurrence within the same document are fairly rare, while lower frequencies of co-occurrence are quite common. We can also see that there are many cases where the two terms occur independently as well. These findings do not yield any great epiphanies, but more important is what the graph does not show: no evidence of outliers or anomalies that might skew our results.

The "lm" function name stands for "linear model" and is the most common way of creating a regression model in R. We embedded the "lm" function within a function called "abline," which adds a line to a plot. Here, we have added a regression line to the plot, to more clearly show that there is a positive relationship between the terms "Web" and "site."

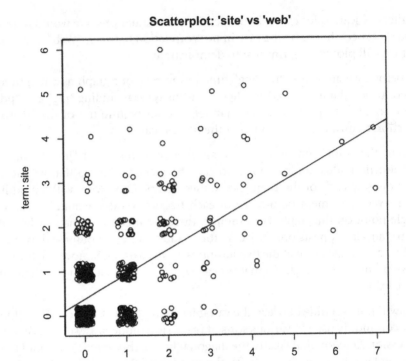

FIGURE 6.2
Strong evidence of frequent co-occurrence of the terms, "web," and "site," with little evidence of any unexpected anomalies.

```
> #Create a scatterplot comparing "site" and "web"
> png("Figure2.png")
> plot(jitter(d[,"site"])~jitter(d[,"web"]), main="Scatterplot:
'site' vs 'web'",xlab="term: web", ylab="term: site")
> abline(lm(d[,"site"]~d[,"web"]))
> dev.off()
```

Cluster Analysis

Suppose we wish to determine which reported incidents are related and group them together. Such groupings may reveal patterns that might be difficult to spot otherwise. This kind of analysis is referred to as "cluster analysis." Two common types of cluster analysis are "hierarchical clustering" and "k-means" clustering.

Hierarchical clustering groups data by finding groupings that maximize the differences between them. K-means clustering groups data by partitioning the data elements in a predefined number of groupings, a parameter commonly referred to as "k" groupings. K-means minimizes the sum of squares distances from each data element to each group's centerpoint.

K-means is very useful for assigning each data element a group member-ship value. In other words, we can create a new column in our data, which provides a group number that each element is placed within. A common problem with k-means, however, is figuring out how many groupings, "k," to specify in advance. Hierarchical clustering is useful for this purpose and can be used in combination with k-means. Once we have decided how many cluster groupings make sense in our data through the use of hierarchical clus-tering, we can perform k-means clustering to assign the groupings. While it is possible to also assign groupings using hierarchical clustering, k-means is less computationally intensive for this process and is often preferred for larger data sets.

The following code sample generates a hierarchical cluster, using the "hclust" function. Notice that we used the "dist" function within the "hclust" function, in order to calculate the differences between the data elements. The result of running the "hclust" is stored in a variable, "hClust." This variable is then plot-ted using R's generic "plot" function.

As an aside, you may have noticed that the "plot" function adjusts its output and graph types depending upon the data that it receives. The "plot" function automatically knows, in this case, that it needs to plot a hierarchical cluster in a tree type of a diagram, known as a "dendogram."

```
> #Hierarchical cluster analysis
> png("Figure3.png")
> hClust <- hclust(dist(dtm))
> plot(hClust, labels=FALSE)
> dev.off()
```

We can see in the resulting dendogram of the hierarchical cluster in Figure 6.3 that there are many levels of groupings. We want to try to choose a level that produces groupings with a fairly good representation of data elements in each. We see that, the second level at the top of the tree is split into three groupings. The first grouping, on the far left, results in very sparse member-ship, if you follow that fork down to its end points. These endpoints are known as "leaf nodes." Each leaf node relates to an individual data element or row. The next grouping to the right at the second level, indicated by the next vertical line at that level, has more data elements within it. The third grouping, however, has by far the most data elements. Choosing to use three clusters appears to offer a relatively good balance between interpretability and group representation.

The choice as to how many clusters to use is highly subjective, and is a balance between trying to gain good representation of data points in each cluster, with having enough clusters to find meaningful relationships in the data. Basically, too few clusters may lack meaningful detail, while too many clusters can be impossible to interpret.

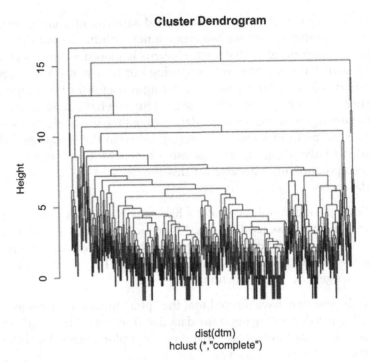

FIGURE 6.3
Dendogram of the document-term matrix.

Based on our hierarchical cluster analysis, we will choose a "k" number of groupings equal to three for our k-means cluster analysis. We use the "kmeans" function on our document-term matrix, "dtm," and set the "centers" parameter to three. We then store the results in a variable we call, "kmClust." We can see the results stored in "kmClust" by either entering "kmClust" on a line by itself or by using the "print" function. Either method does the same thing, but some feel that using the "print" function is more explicit and readable in the code. This time, we use the "print" function just to demonstrate it. Notice that the results indicate how many members are within each cluster. The results are a bit different than with hierarchical clustering and the methods differ. However, hierarchical clustering can still provide a good estimate for the purposes of guessing a decent value for "k." There is, however, one cluster that has far fewer members than the other two; albeit it appears to have more members than the smallest cluster given by the hierarchical method. The representation of data elements in each cluster looks decent overall, though.

Only a sample of the output is shown, as the cluster means is given for each and every term in the data-term matrix in the actual output. Also, every incident row in the data is assigned a cluster membership value. Again, only a portion of the membership output is shown due to size constraints on the page. Lastly, the output includes some diagnostic statistics, regarding the sum of squares fit, and the available values that can be extracted from the output. See the help for the "kmeans" function for additional details on these.

```
> kmClust <- kmeans(dtm,centers=3)
> print(kmClust)
K-means clustering with 3 clusters of sizes 216, 264, 83
Cluster means:
access attack can data hacked...
1 0.07407407 0.1111111 0.06018519 0.15740741 0.1203704
2 0.20454545 0.3977273 0.14393939 0.07954545 0.2727273
3 0.10843373 0.5301205 0.28915663 0.38554217 0.3614458
...
Clustering vector:
1 2 3 4 5 6 7 8 9 10 11 12 13 14...
2 2 2 2 2 2 2 2  2  2  2  2  2
...
Within cluster sum of squares by cluster:
[1] 1194.569 2160.356 1744.482
(between_SS/total_SS = 16.3%)

Available components:
[1] "cluster" "centers" "totss" "withinss" "tot.withinss"
[6] "betweenss" "size"
```

We can now append the cluster memberships as an additional value to our data-term matrix. The sample code below creates a new data frame that combines "dtm" data-term matrix, with the cluster members by calling the "cluster" component from the cluster results stored in the "kmClust" object we created. Notice how we use the dollar sign in R to call a specific component from the list of components available in the output. Again, the list of available components is shown at the end of the previous k-means output that we discussed. You can see "cluster" in that list.

```
> #Assign cluster membership to the original data
> dtmWithClust <- data.frame(inspect(dtm), kmClust$cluster)
```

Now, we can print the "dtmWithClust" data frame object we just created, and see how the additional last column containing the cluster memberships was appended. In this case, the first five documents all belong to cluster number three.

```
> print(dtmWithClust)
Docs access attack can data hacked...kmClust.cluster
1 2 0 0 0 1...3
2 0 1 0 0 1...3
3 0 0 0 0 0...3
4 0 2 0 0 0...3
5 0 1 0 0 0...3
...
```

With the cluster memberships assigned, we can use this information to build a predictive model to categorize new hacking reports that are entered into the Web Hacking Information Database. Of course, we may want to know how to generalize characteristics that tend to define each cluster. That can be a bit of a challenge with each word in our document-term matrix representing a predictive variable. Some methods that can be helpful in this include decision tree classification analysis using the "rpart" function or the "randomForests" function. The "randomForests" function combines the results of many decision tree classifiers. This function is found within the "randomForest" package. A detailed discussion into decision tree analysis gets into another realm of data mining and is beyond the scope of this chapter. However, we show a random forest example below.

Before running this example, you will need to be sure that you have the "randomForest" package installed and that the library is initiated. We show these steps first. Notice in specifying the model in the "randomForest" function that we use the tilde along with a period. Again, the tilde can be read as "by," and the period as "all other variables." Thus, our model specification of "kmClust.cluster~." can be read as "classify the cluster variable by all other variables." The "importance=TRUE" parameter specifies to output a list of all of the predictive variables and their relative importance as classifiers. In this case, the output shows all of the words, along with statistics giving each word's relative importance. The larger the number, the more important the word is in characterizing each incident within a cluster.

```
> install.packages("randomForest", dependencies=TRUE)
...
> library("randomForest")

...
> rfClust <- randomForest(kmClust.cluster~., data=dtmWithClust,
importance=TRUE, proximity=TRUE)
Warning message:
In randomForest.default(m, y,...):
The response has five or fewer unique values. Are you sure you want
to do regression?
> print(rfClust)

Call:
randomForest(formula = kmClust.cluster ~., data = dtmWithClust,
importance = TRUE, proximity = TRUE)
Type of random forest: regression
Number of trees: 500
No. of variables tried at each split: 10

Mean of squared residuals: 0.05231353
% Var explained: 90.23
> importance(rfClust)
```

```
%IncMSE IncNodePurity
access              5.21554027 2.1754015
attack              0.73614019 2.2021336
can                -0.43914970 1.2053006
data                2.12488252 1.3255387
hacked             -2.22153755 3.0291678
hacker              0.59934964 2.1058682
hackers            -0.69140487 1.4719546
incident            9.35312755 6.7942922
information         0.92171115 1.9432987
informationp        1.10089894 1.3157080
injection           0.98117200 1.4235802
new                 1.89448271 2.0425851
one                -1.38418946 1.8823775
online              1.13857428 0.9484073
padditional         1.87159685 0.7986896
ppadditional        2.35617800 0.9213330
said                7.12029542 1.8712096
security           -0.84890151 2.2249081
service            -2.18474469 0.4115085
site              101.31981296 144.1131055
sites               5.38968388 5.5126839
sql                 1.97680424 2.0980965
time                0.05651688 2.7443020
used               -1.26504782 1.3189609
users              -2.15274360 0.9221132
using               0.67911496 2.0038781
vulnerability      -0.42220017 1.5492946
web                60.89116556 92.5641831
Website             4.98273660 1.4276663
xss                 4.11442275 1.6486677
```

OTHER APPLICABLE SECURITY AREAS AND SCENARIOS

We used rather generic data, but these same techniques can be applied to a variety of security scenarios. It is difficult to get actual data pertaining to real security breaches, as such data sets tend to be proprietary. Also, company leaders generally are not keen to release their data to the public. Such proprietary data sets often contain personally identifiable information that maybe difficult to remove entirely. They also can reveal weaknesses in a company's defenses, which maybe exploited by other attackers. The data used in this chapter does not reveal the full extent of the power of the text analysis tools in R as would actual, detailed corporate data.

Nevertheless, it is hoped that the analysis provided here is sufficient to get readers thinking and using their own creativity as to how to use these methods on their own data. Following are a few suggestions to think about, in hopes that they will be a catalyst for further creativity in the readers.

Additional Security Scenarios for Text Mining

Most call centers record the telephone conversations that they have with their customers. These can provide a breadcrumb trail as to the patterns and techniques used by social hackers. Social engineering involves coaxing people into giving up security-related information, such as usernames, passwords, account numbers, and credit card details, generally by falsely impersonating a legitimate stakeholder. These recordings may be bulk transformed into text by using automated voice dictation software, such as the Dragonfly package in Python (http://code.google.com/p/dragonfly/). Some call centers utilize chat sessions, or e-mail instead of phone calls, in which case voice to text conversion would be unnecessary. Text mining techniques maybe used to find patterns in the resulting text files with each call representing a document. In addition to applying the same processes as discussed in this chapter, you might also have call center employees flag each call in the database that seem suspicious. You could use decision trees such as discussed in this chapter to find combinations of words that may predict a high probability of fraudulent intent from a caller. Even if a caller uses different phone numbers to make phone calls, which is a common technique among social engineers, the word patterns they use may give them away.

Another potential use of text mining is with log files, such as from network routers or server logs, such as those we analyzed in Chapter 3. In that chapter, we used more direct means of finding potential security breaches and potentially malicious activity. However, text mining techniques could be applied to log data, such as the user, agent, or referrer fields. This could yield patterns that might otherwise be obscured. For instance, a referrer might use several variants of urls from which to make requests of the server. This would be hard to catch with a direct query. However, cluster analysis on word frequencies could find enough similarities in the urls used that they could be found to be associated.

Corporate e-mail contains very large collections of unstructured text. Most corporations have software that helps them sift through e-mails to identify spam. However, it is more unusual to find systems that identify phishing attacks. Text mining could be used to find patterns in phishing attack e-mails, and predictive models could be used to identify new e-mails that have a high probability of being a phishing attack. Predictive models could include the decision trees discussed here, or any number of a wide variety of other predictive modeling algorithms that are beyond the scope of this text. Once potential new phishing attack threats are identified, employees could be warned about them as a training measure and the senders could be placed on a watch list. If suspicious e-mail senders identified by the algorithms are later verified as actual attackers, they could be put on a block list, preventing further e-mails from getting through. Of course, there are ways to get around this, such as through bots that send e-mails from multiple accounts. Never-ending vigilance is required.

Text Mining and Big Data

When data sets to be analyzed become too big to be handled by analytical tools such as R, there are a variety of techniques that can be applied. Some techniques are used to turn big data into smaller data through aggregation, so that it can be more readily digested by analytical tools such as R. Hadoop and MapReduce, as discussed in Chapter 3, were used in a similar manner, to aggregate a large amount of data into a much smaller time series, which was then analyzed in R as well as a spreadsheet.

Similar aggregation and data size reduction techniques can be used for text mining, although you will need a means of tokenizing the data. That is, you will need some way of isolating each word occurrence and pairing it with an occurrence frequency for each document. We discussed Hive as a means of using familiar SQL-like code to aggregate data. Hive happens to also have several built-in functions for tokenizing data. For basic application of a stop word list, and calculation of word frequencies, the "ngrams" function in Hive is very useful. This function also has the capability of only selecting words that occur above a frequency threshold, further reducing the size of the data. Another interesting Hive function for string tokenizing is "context_ngrams," which tokenizes data within a sentence context. For instance, you might want to only find words that occur within the context of a sentence containing the words "username" and "password." If you want more information and examples as to the usage of these functions, you are encouraged to examine Apache's resources online such as the Apache wiki: https://cwiki.apache.org/confluence/display/Hive/StatisticsAndDataMining.

Once the data are tokenized and reduced to more manageable size, the previously discussed analytical methods can be applied in R. The R language has a vast number of analytical packages and functions of all sorts, including others for text mining that we do not have space to cover here. So, it makes sense to try and do much of your analysis using R if you can.

Alternatively, instead of aggregating and reducing your data size, another means of handling Big Data is to run your analytical algorithms utilizing parallel processing. There are many ways to do this, although many may add significant additional complexity to your processes and code. The CRAN R Web site at http://www.cran.r-project.org has an entire page listing and describing R packages for utilizing parallel processing with R. This page can be found by clicking the "Task Views" link in the left margin of the CRAN R Web site, followed by selecting the "HighPerformanceComputing" link. In addition to packages that run R on multiple processors, such as "multicore" and "snow," there are also packages for running R jobs in a Hadoop, MapReduce framework such as "HadoopStreaming," as well as Revolution Analytics' "rmr" package. Before further investigating Big Data techniques, however, you should be sure you understand the foundational text mining concepts provided in the examples in this chapter.

## CHAPTER 7

Security Intelligence and Next Steps

INFORMATION IN THIS CHAPTER:

- Overview (17 pages)
- Security Intelligence
  - Basic Security Intelligence Analysis
  - Business Extension of Security Intelligence
- Security Breaches
- Practical Applications
  - Insider Threat
  - Resource Justification
  - Risk Management
  - Challenges
    - Data
    - Integration of Equipment and Personnel
    - False Positives
- Concluding Remarks

OVERVIEW

In the previous chapters we provided an overview of the data and analysis steps of the security analytics process. In this chapter, we will explain how you develop security intelligence so that you may increase your security response posture. See Figure 7.1 for the security analytics process. The goal of this chapter is to provide you with the knowledge to apply what we have discussed in this book and to address the next steps to implementing security analytics in your organization.

SECURITY INTELLIGENCE

We want to develop security intelligence so that we can make accurate and timely decisions to respond to threats. Although security intelligence may seem like the newest buzzword people are using when talking about using security analytics,

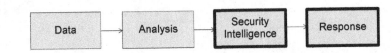

FIGURE 7.1
Security analytics process.

there is no clear definition of what exactly security intelligence entails. So, let us start with a discussion about the differences between information and intelligence. Information is raw data (think of it as your log files), whereas intelligence is analyzed and refined material (think of it as the result from looking through your log files and finding an anomaly). Intelligence provides you with the means to take action by aiding you in your decision-making and reducing your security risk. In other words, intelligence is processed information allowing you to address a threat. By generating security intelligence using the tools discussed in this book, you will be better prepared to respond to threats to your organization.

Basic Security Intelligence Analysis

Security intelligence is especially relevant because experts have found that companies failed to identify a security breach until a third party notified the companies, even though they had evidence of the intrusion in their log files. We all know that it is impossible to review every log file collected, but with security analytics, you will be able to set up your tools to help you to identify and prioritize security action items. While you still may be dealing with historical data, you are able to optimize your response time to incidents by quickly converting your raw data into security intelligence.

Once you have your security intelligence, you have two options: take action or take no action. You would think that the most obvious option is to take action to address your threat, but security intelligence is often tricky because things are not always as "clear-cut" as we would like them to be. Sometimes, your intelligence is the "smoking gun" identifying a security incident. For example, in the case where you find "two concurrent virtual private network (VPN) logins" or "two VPN logins from different parts of the country," you would probably call the employee and ask about the suspicious logins. In the best case scenario, the employee may have a completely legitimate reason for the logins from two different IP addresses. In the worst case scenario, the employee's credentials have been compromised. Either way, you will be able to quickly mitigate the potential threat (unauthorized access).

Other times, the intelligence you found is just an indicator of something bigger that you have not quite figured out yet. For example, the intelligence you identified may be an indicator of a hacker, who is in the reconnaissance phase, sending probing packets to your network ports to observe the response. More often than not, it may just be an unexplained anomaly or a false positive for which you will find no answers. Such is the nature of working with intelligence—you never have complete visibility of the threat actors or their actions, but you still must do your best to protect your organization.

Security intelligence is oftentimes used for explanatory analysis (or retrospective analysis) to determine what happened during a security incident so that steps can be taken to mitigate a threat. Exploratory analysis is very valuable to increasing an organization's defenses. Yet, the ultimate goal with security intelligence is to be able to conduct predictive analysis: to guess what your attacker will do so that you can implement countermeasures to thwart your attacker. Predictive analysis may seem more relevant in a real-time incident, such as ongoing distributed denial of service (DDOS) or a live intrusion. However, it is also relevant for dealing with day-to-day situations: by knowing your environment and your operational baseline, you are able to identify your strengths and weaknesses, which will assist you in developing responsive strategies.

It is impossible to protect against every threat, so one way to address this is by knowing your organization's landscape and your intelligence gaps, which are the areas in which you lack information on your threats. By understanding your intelligence gaps, you will be able to focus your efforts to address these gaps and to set up early warning sensors. These sensors are usually a combination of tools to include vendor solutions (e.g., security information and event management) and the security analytics techniques discussed in this book.

Additionally, you will be able to address your internal security gaps. For example, suppose you know that your antivirus (AV) vendor's product is not as robust as you would like, but your budget does not allow you to purchase a better product. Knowing that this is one of your intelligence gaps, you may be more vigilant at reviewing your logs and at checking your quarantine e-mail. You may be also looking for information to cover this gap through other means (increasing security education or frequent system tests).

As you develop your organization's security intelligence, you will have a better understanding of your organization's threat landscape and you will develop greater confidence in your ability to respond to the threats. Once you start using security intelligence, your mind-set changes from "reacting to events" to "methodically addressing top threats." Our goal in this section is to have you start thinking about how security intelligence can increase your overall effectiveness and productivity. To cover all aspects of intelligence analysis in this section was not possible, but we hope to give you a basic understanding of how it works and how it can help you. If you are interested in learning more about this topic, you will find a resource by searching the Internet for "security intelligence analysis" or "intelligence analysis."

Business Extension of Security Analytics

There is no doubt that your organization already collects data for different business processes (marketing, accounting, operations, network management, etc.). However, most organizations conduct data analysis using standard analysis methods (i.e., spreadsheets) from their databases; therefore, they have yet to harness the power of analytics.

We provided you with the knowledge to conduct an analysis of your existing security data to extract intelligence for security decisions by using the powerful, open-source software tools to examine structured and unstructured data. If you expand this to all of your organization's businesses processes, you will be able to examine data in ways that you could never have imagined. You will be able to do this in real time to make proactive business decisions, instead of just using historical data to make reactive decisions. In fact, the real power of analytics is realized when you are able to take data across different departments to generate predictive security intelligence. The techniques we cover may also be applied to any of your organization's business processes—it is just a matter of expanding your skillset and applying the proper techniques to the right data set.

SECURITY BREACHES

As you start examining your data, it is inevitable that you will discover a security incident; thus, we would be remiss if we did not touch upon the steps to take when you have identified a security incident. If your organization has a preexisting security incident response policy in place, you would naturally follow those procedures. For those who do not have established policies or procedures, we encourage you to begin creating a plan to address the key phases of incident response: prepare, notify, analyze, mitigate, and recovery. As a starting point, there is a plethora of security policy samples that you can find by searching the Internet for "security policy templates" or for a specific type of security policy (information security, network security, mobile security, etc.).

Depending on the severity of the intrusion, you may want to consider hiring forensic and/or intrusion-response experts to assist you with a security breach investigation and to identify procedures to protect against future intrusions. You may also have legally mandated reporting requirements to federal or state authorities and/or risk management reporting requirements, which will depend on the type of data compromised (intellectual property, personal identifying information, etc.). In addition, you may need to seek legal counsel to determine if law enforcement reporting is necessary. We encourage you to develop these procedures now and to conduct "table-top" (e.g., dry run) exercises, so that in the event of an incident, you are able to quickly respond.

PRACTICAL APPLICATION

Insider Threat

When we look at security, we often focus on threats external to our organization, rather than internal to the organization, because the probability of a threat coming from the outside seems greater than one coming from the inside. However, while less likely to occur, an insider oftentimes causes more harm to a company than an external threat could because an insider knows how you operate and where your keep your valuable information. So, let us start by examining a scenario with an insider threat.

The owners of a small, start-up company found it strange when several of their programmers quit the company at the same time. When company executives "got wind" that the individuals had gone to work for a competitor, they began to ask questions about whether or not the company's intellectual property had been stolen, since these programmers were working on key pieces of their product. Since this was a small company, the management did not have a security officer, so they looked to the IT personnel to examine the problem and to look for evidence. The first area the IT personnel examined was the e-mail of the employees. Through the e-mail, they were able to piece together that the employees who left the company were collaborating and they intended to steal the code they developed at this company. These e-mails were key evidence that the company saved to an external storage device for preservation. The company made a secondary copy so that they could review the data.

Once the e-mails are preserved, rather than manually reading through the e-mails, you could use the text mining technique covered in this book to see if you can identify patterns that are not readily apparent, such as other associates involved in the source-code theft and when they initiated the plan to steal the code. You may also find other clues, which may cause you to expand your investigation. For example, the former employees in our scenario continued to correspond with current employees at the company even after they left the company. The company was able to identify the personal e-mail accounts of the former employees because they forwarded e-mail to themselves prior to quitting. From the e-mail accounts, the company was able to determine that they were still e-mailing current employees. One of the current employees, who had not left the company yet, was involved in the source-code theft and was still feeding the former employees with details about how the company knew of the theft and still providing insider information.

To expand upon this scenario, for the sake of showing you further applications, let us say you were able to determine that one of the former employee physically downloaded the source code onto a removable USB device on a particular date. What types of security data would law enforcement need from your organization? First, the system used to download the data would have important evidence of the USB device connections, to include artifacts in the registry keys (link files, USB removable devices connected to the system, timeline information, etc.). Second, showing that the employee was physically present in the building would be beneficial to building your case. Other areas to examine would include employee access logs (building entry, parking entry, computer logins, etc.). If you are lucky enough to have physical access log data to your building, you could run security analytics on employee patterns to identify anomalies—which may or may not serve as an indicator of when the criminal activity began. While video surveillance data will provide you with additional evidence to support your case, current techniques in video analytics have not yet fully developed—robust tools that can handle large amounts of data from multiple video feeds and conduct facial recognition at a granular level are still being developed.

A final consideration in our insider threat scenario that we will discuss, which is often overlooked because companies do not expect it to occur, is an unauthorized access after the employee has resigned. Sometimes a company's IT department may not remove accesses to systems immediately, thereby offering a way for the employee to return to the company. Or, in the case where a former employee, who managed the IT network or was technically sophisticated, may leave a backdoor from which the employee may access the company's system. Why is it important to examine these areas? Besides the obvious point that it poses a threat to the organization, if you can show that the employee accessed the company's system while no longer employed, you are able to show another form of criminal activity—unauthorized access. An Internet search for "mitigating insider threats" will provide you with additional resources and ideas to better protect your organization.

Finally, you must also consider the situation in which an employee's credentials were stolen. Should you call the person and start asking questions or should you just report it to your management? This highlights the importance of having an incident response plan—it assists you in knowing what steps to take and when to involve your management. Depending on your organization's policy and management decisions, the next steps could include any of following: consult with legal counsel or human resources personnel, interview the employee, or notify your board of directors. Inaction is also action—your company may choose to do nothing, which tends to be common in smaller organizations. After determining if there was any wrongdoing by the employee, your management could also opt to pursue criminal enforcement and/or civil litigation.

Resource Justification

There is a great difference between telling your management that the number of security incidents is increasing and showing your management a simulation tool depicting intrusion attempts during a certain time period. In the former example, your management probably will not grasp the significance of the threat or the impact to your organization. In the latter example, your management can see the rapid increase of attempts and better comprehend the scope of the threats. It is often the case where management cannot understand the impact of security incidents because it seems far removed from everyday business processes. Thus, they only seem concerned with security when an incident is identified because they expect you to protect the organization. Security analytics can help you to elevate your management's security awareness by providing you with ways to transform your data into easily understood security intelligence, thereby bringing security information up to their level of comprehension.

Security analytics can also support your justification for resources. By using the techniques covered in this book, you can support your claim for resources to support your security initiatives. For example, if you want to justify the need to purchase a new intrusion detection system, you can easily do so by first showing the statistics on the growth of the threats within your organization's network. This coupled with the identification of what the current system is not identifying (intelligence gaps) and a simulation of the effects from not identifying the threats translates your security concern into a business problem. Your management may be more inclined to pay for a system to support security, even when there are competing business interests, because you are able to show a compelling need. Most importantly, you are able to translate how this compelling need affects your organization's profits and/or productivity. You could also use this technique to justify hiring more security personnel and to change internal business practices and/or policies.

Risk Management

A big concern with the use of analytics is the collection and use of sensitive data. There is always the risk of inadvertently exposing sensitive data, no matter what policies are in place. We simply cannot be prepared for every type of security response because the threat of malicious attacks continues to increase unabated. Moreover, the trend for allowing "personal devices" to be used in the workplace (also known as Bring Your Own Device (BYOD)) creates an even more complex risk management situation because sensitive data can now reside on these devices. When you add the trend of sharing the analytics data with partners and suppliers to increase collaboration and innovation, the risks escalates even more because now the sensitive data reside outside of your organization.

The ability to collect large volumes of data containing sensitive personal, financial, or medical information places a greater social responsibility upon those using analytics. No matter where the data reside (in the cloud or within an organization), a security practitioner should be acutely aware of the risks associated with data reuse, sharing, and ownership. Therefore, you need to know the types of data you are handling, so you may take the appropriate steps to safeguard the data through information management and organizational poli-cies. Additionally, if you are working with other individuals handling the data, they should be trained on how to safeguard the data and the ethics of properly using the data.

One way to protect the data is to use data anonymizing tools prior to or after conducting analytics processes. You can do this by using the techniques pro-vided in Chapter 5, through the use of a script, to convert the data of concern into anonymized data. In addition, once your organization determines the need to involve law enforcement or to pursue civil litigation, you may be given the responsibility to produce the evidence supporting the incident. Prior to disclosing the information, you should review the data for any sensitive infor-mation, such as personally identifiable information, financial data (i.e., credit cards and bank accounts), Health Insurance Portability and Accountability Act and Gramm–Leach–Bliley Act protected data, and intellectual property. Your legal counsel will be able to provide you with more details on other data need-ing special protection.

Challenges

We realize that there are many challenges to using security analytics, since the field is still evolving and people are still trying to figure out how to effectively implement the techniques in their organization. If you are reading this book, you probably are not considering using a vendor for your security analytics; therefore, you may be thinking of the logistics involved with implementing it within your organization.

Data

When it relates to data, you should consider two aspects: identifying the "right" data and normalizing the data. First, you will need to examine the security-related data collected within your organization. Most people think of network, mail, and firewall logs when you mention data collection for security; however, other peripheral log files (e.g., building access, telephone, and VPN logs) are also relevant. You will need to assess if the data you are collecting is relevant to achieving your goals as a security practitioner. If you are not collecting the "right" data, no matter what types of security analytics tools are used, you will not produce actionable intelligence.

One way to identify which logs are important for your organization is by looking at what is on your network that must be protected (your organization's "crown jewels") from the perspective of an attacker. For example, a bank's "crown jew-els" would be the customer and bank financial data and a software company's "crown jewels" would be its source code. One way to access the "crown jew-els" is through a back-office server, which is accessed by an employee's desktop computer via e-mail. Another way to access the "crown jewels" is through the

Web server in the demilitarized zone (DMZ), from which a database behind the firewall is accessed to get to the back-office server. Therefore, all of the processes related to accessing the "crown jewels" should be considered your critical log files. These log files should be collected and analyzed using security analytics.

Now that you have the "right" data, you need to normalize the data before transforming it into security intelligence. Normalization techniques are used to arrange the data into logical groupings and to minimize data redundancy. Conversely, it may be necessary to denormalize the data structure to enable faster querying, but the downside is that there will be data redundancies and loss in flexibility. To normalize or denormalize the data, you could use the Hadoop and MapReduce tools, but it would involve writing a program. An Internet search for normalization or denormalization techniques or programs will provide you with more in-depth information.

We stress in this book the need for you to use security analytics on your data so that you have an idea of your organization's baseline. For example, your baseline could include IP address logins via VPN from the Philippines because your company outsourced the development of a specific function to a company located there. This baseline could trigger you to conduct more monitoring of the VPN from the Philippines (because you feel this is a higher risk to your network) or it may allow you to direct your resources to other threat areas because you are confident that the logins pose a lower threat.

Integration of Equipment and Personnel

In implementing security analytics, it will be necessary to integrate a data warehouse into your existing architecture. This is no easy task, as there are many considerations in collecting data from various sources and integrating the data into a data warehouse using the extraction, transformation, and loading process. Designing a data warehouse is out of the scope for this book; however, we have listed a few questions to consider as a starting point.

- Will this data warehouse contain an SQL or a NoSQL database?
- Will the data reside in the cloud or on your organization's network?
- What are the risks involved with protecting the data?
- Do you have enough storage capacity?
- Do you have robust servers and how does the location of your data affect your server performance?
- What type of schema model (star, snowflake, etc.) will you use?

The security analytics tools will help you to generate security information, but you need the skilled personnel to interpret and transform the information into security intelligence. However, there is a critical shortage of cybersecurity practitioners and analytics professionals, and this trend is expected to continue for the foreseeable future. Even if you are working for a large organization with the resources to hire security analytics personnel, it will be difficult to staff your team with experienced personnel. You will most likely have to train personnel to evolve into the security analytics roles.

False Positives

As you begin to use security analytics, you may notice high false-positive rates or that you are not seeing what you thought you would see. It may be necessary for you to adjust your strategy to accommodate your data. For example, let us say that you are looking at end-user domain name server (DNS) lookups to identify possible malicious activity of an attacker who has compromised your system. You are wanting to do this because you suspect there could be an advanced persistent threat in your network. Therefore, you are searching for evidence that DNS manipulation is being used to hide the IP addresses of remote servers or is being used as a covert channel for data exfiltration. The assumption in conducting this analysis is that an attacker would have a higher DNS lookup rate when compared to your average user's DNS lookup rate. You find that your initial analysis reveals a lot of false positives. If you shift your strategy by looking at second-level domains, removing internationalized domain names, or using a public suffix list (also known as effective top-level domain list), you may obtain better results.

You may also run into a situation where after adjusting your strategy, you still do not find any security incidents. It is at this time that you will need to view your results using a "different lens" to search for meaning in what you have already found. In going back to the DNS lookup scenario, perhaps even after you have shifted your strategy, you still cannot seem to find malicious DNS lookups. Let us look at what you have—a list of your organization's DNS lookups, which is baseline over a certain period of time. As we have stressed before, this information is very important in security—you must know your organization's baseline before you can detect anomalies. In addition, you have also identified the DNS lookups, so you could run these domain names against a domain watch list to check that there are no suspicious lookups. We want to stress that what may initially seem like a dead end, may actually be an opportunity—security intelligence of your organization or your threat landscape. Once you have figured out the security intelligence of importance to your organization, you can automate these tasks to assist you in protecting your organization. This is the beauty of security analytics.

CONCLUDING REMARKS

Our goal with this book was to demonstrate how security practitioners may use open-source technologies to implement security analytics in the workplace. We are confident that you are already well on your way to developing your organization's security intelligence with the techniques we covered in this book. Most importantly, we encourage you to use security analytics to increase your organization's overall security, thereby reducing risks and security breaches. While you may initially find yourself using security analytics to do specific tasks (i.e., reduce enterprise costs and identify anomalies), as your sophistication with analytics grows, we believe you will see many more applications for the techniques. As you begin to implement security analytics in your organization, your efforts to increase security will become more apparent. Rather than using a traditional, reactive model of security, you will be implementing a proactive model of security. Specifically, security analytics should contribute to developing your security intelligence.

Learning the tools presented in this book is the starting point of your security analytics journey. We have given you several techniques to add to your tool kit, but we hope that you expand your knowledge. As analytics is a rapidly expanding field, you will, indeed, have no shortage of proprietary or open-source technologies to learn. In fact, open-source technologies may outpace proprietary software!

We challenge you to "think outside the box" and to look for ways to integrate security analytics solutions in your organization. The possibilities for applying the techniques are endless. More importantly, you will be providing your organization with value-added intelligence to answer questions it never knew could be answered using the data your organization already collects.

We are convinced that these security analytics tools are extremely effective. We also believe that if more organizations utilized these open-source tools, they would be better prepared to protect their organization by spotting an activity while it is occurring, rather than responding to an event after-the-fact. Good luck on your journey!

Index

Note: Page numbers followed by "f" and "t" indicate figures and tables respectively.

A

Access analytics
  argparse module, 109
  csv module, 109–110
  datetime module, 110
  haversine distance, 116–117
  "Havesine Python,", 117
  Linux/Unix systems, 110
  math module, 110
  MaxMind GeoIP API, 116
  MaxMind's GeoIP module, 121
  parse_args() function, 112
  parser.add.argument method, 112
  pseudocode, 116
  Python, 100, 103
    Codecademy, 103–104
    resources, 103
    Web site, 104
  re module, 109
  remote access Python analytics
    program flow, 111, 111f
  result analysis
    connections types, 121
    haversine distance, 118–119
    malicious remote connections
      identification, 121
    User8 access behavior, 119,
      119f
    User90 access behavior, 119,
      120f
    User91 access behavior, 120,
      120f
    vpn.csv file, output, 117, 118f
  scripting language, 102
  third-party remote access, 100
  unauthorized access, 100
  unauthorized remote access
    identification

anomalous user connections,
    105–107
  credit card transaction
    statements, 105
  data collection, 105, 106f
  data processing, 108–109
  Haversine distances, 107–108
VPN
  add-on two-factor authenti-
    cation mechanisms, 101
  CONNECT variable, 115
  Event class, 114–115
  logs, 112–113
  monitoring, 101–102
  normalize() function, 113–114
  public network, 101
  "RawMessage" column, 114
  "ReceiveTime" column, 114
  tunneling protocols, 100
  unsecured/untrusted network,
    100
Aggregate function, 136
Amazon's Elastic MapReduce
  environment, 29
Analytical software and tools
  Arena. *See* Arena
  big data, 15–16
  GUI, 13
  Python, 19–20
  R language. *See* R language
  statistical programming, 14–15
Analytics
  access analytics. *See* Access
    analytics
  authentication, 9
  big data, 5–6
  computer systems and networks,
    4–5

expert system program, 10
free-form text data, 8
incident response, 7. *See also*
  Incident response
intrusion detection, 7
knowledge engineering, 4, 10
Known Unknowns, 8
log files, 5
logical access controls, 9
machine learning, 2
multiple large data centers, 5
security breaches and attacks, 1
security processes, 8–9
simulation-based decisions, 9
simulations, 4, 8–9
statistical techniques, 2
supervised learning, 2–3
text mining, 4
unauthorized access attempts, 10
Unknown Unknowns, 8
unsupervised learning, 3–4
virus/malware infection, 9
VPN access, 10
vulnerability management, 11–12
ApacheLogData files, 27
Apache Mahout, 14
Arena
  adding data and parameters, 21, 69
  conceptual model creation, 21, 68
  flowchart modules, 21
  IT service desk ticket queue, 68, 68f
  Microsoft Visio, 68
  Model window flowchart view,
    20, 67
  Model window spreadsheet view,
    20, 68
  Project bar, 20, 67
  Rockwell Automation, 20, 67

Printed in the United States
By Bookmasters